Preface

Students across the nation have been using the Speaking Solutions Nift to learn speech and handwriting recognition skills since 2002. We are proud to introduce our newest speech recognition training manual "Speech Recognition Applications: The Basics and Beyond."

Speech recognition technology has made numerous advancements over the past decade and has become easier to use and much more efficient. Speech recognition software is now being used by more and more individuals in a wide variety of industries and professional careers every day. Most people can create documents using speech recognition software much faster than they can type. By learning to use speech as an alternate input method, students and professionals will increase their overall productivity and acquire a valuable skill that will give them a competitive edge as they advance in their education and careers.

About this Book

Speech Recognition Applications: The Basics and Beyond provides step-by-step directions for getting started with speech recognition software. It also provides instruction in developing the basic speech recognition skills needed to dictate, correct, edit and format a variety of documents. Exercises are included for navigating the Internet by voice and creating e-mails; using Microsoft Word to create letters, reports, tables and macros; and using Microsoft Excel for creating spreadsheets.

The unique design of this book offers a perfect training solution for students, teachers, and business professionals. It offers easy to follow lessons with step-by-step directions and many screen shots and tips. The exercises will help you learn how to use speech recognition as a daily input device and will help you improve your overall speed and accuracy.

This book focuses on the new features of Dragon NaturallySpeaking® (version 12) because Dragon NaturallySpeaking® is currently the industry leader for speech recognition. However, the concepts and exercises presented could also be used for other speech recognition software programs. All lessons and exercises are compatible with Microsoft Office XP, 2003, 2007 and 2010; and Internet Explorer, Mozilla Firefox and Chrome.

Learning outcomes

When you have completed this book, you will be able to demonstrate mastery of speech recognition skills, which includes:
- creating and managing a speech profile
- properly using microphone
- using correct commands
- navigating, formatting, correcting, editing, saving and printing by voice
- dictating at over 100 words a minute at 98% accuracy or above
- preparing correctly formatted documents including e-mail messages, letters, reports, tables and spreadsheets

System Requirements for Dragon NaturallySpeaking 12

- CPU: We recommend 2.2 GHZ Intel dual core or equivalent AMD processor. (Minimum 1 GHz Intel® Pentium® or equivalent AMD processor or 1.66 GHz Intel® Atom® processor). *Faster processors yield fastr performance.* (**IMPORTANT: SSE2 instruction set required**)
- Processor Cache: We recommend 2 MB L2 cache (minimum 512 KB L2 cache)
- Free hard disk space: 3.2 GB (4 GB for localized non-English versions)

Supported Operating Systems:

- Microsoft Windows 7 and higher, 32-bit and 64-bit
- Microsoft Windows Vista SP2, 32-bit and 64-bit
- Microsoft Windows XP SP3, 32-bit only
- Windows Server 2008 SP2 and R2, 32-bit and 64-bit
- RAM: We recommend 2 GB for Windows XP, Windows Vista, Windows 7 and Windows Server 2008 32-bit, *4 GB* for Windows 7 and Windows Server 2008 64-bit. (Minimum 1 GB Windows XP and Windows Vista and 2 GB for Windows 7 and Windows Server 2008).
- Microsoft Internet Explorer 7 or higher (free download at www.microsoft.com)
- Sound card supporting 16-bit recording
- DVD-ROM drive required for installation
- Nuance-approved noise-canceling headset microphone (included in purchase). See details at support.nuance.com/compatibility/ (includes Bluetooth microphones, recorders, and Tablet PCs).

Note: An internet connection is required for product activation (a quick anonymous process).

The Dragon install process checks that your system meets the minimum requirements; if they are not met, Dragon NaturallySpeaking will not be installed and you will receive the following message.

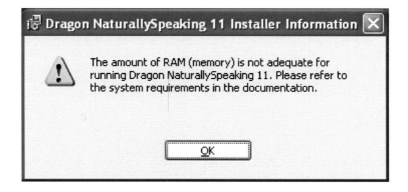

For a limited time, you may be able to still purchase a prior version of Dragon NaturallySpeaking that will work on your current system.

TABLE OF CONTENTS

CHAPTER 9—WEB NAVIGATION/SEARCHES, VOICE SHORTCUTS, & E-MAILS

CHAPTER 10—ENHANCING YOUR PROFILE

CHAPTER 11--REINFORCEMENT ACTIVITIES

CHAPTER 1—LEARNING ABOUT SPEECH RECOGNITION

Speech recognition is one of the most sophisticated technologies ever created for the personal computer. Speech recognition products use the human voice as the main interface between the user and the computer. Speaker–dependent speech recognition systems, such as Dragon NaturallySpeaking® from Nuance Communications, create an individual voice profile for each user of the system. The voice profile contains information about the unique characteristics of each person's voice along with a customized set of words, known as a vocabulary, and user-specific information including software settings and personalized voice commands.

1.1 Speech Recognition Background

Research into this area spans over five decades. The earliest attempts to devise systems for automatic speech recognition were made in the 1950s. Much of the early research leading to the development of speech activation and recognition technology was funded by NSA, NSF and the Defense Department's DARPA in the 1980s.

In 1985, Raymond "Ray" Kurzweil, an American inventor and futurist, introduced the Kurzweil Voice System, the first 1,000-word discrete-speech recognizer. This interface, adaptable to many applications, allowed the user to control the application by voice without modifying the operating system or software. In 1987, Kurzweil introduced the first 20,000-word discrete-speech recognizer, which was incorporated into Kurzweil Voice Report software and allowed users to create structured reports by voice. This speech recognition technology was designed initially for individuals in the disability community.

The early versions of speech recognition products were clunky and hard to use. The early language-recognition systems had to make compromises: they were "tuned" to be dependent on a particular speaker, or had small vocabulary, or used a very stylized and rigid syntax.

In 1994, Kurzweil successfully developed fully operational continuous dictation. This led to the development of continued speech recognition (CSR). Kurzweil Educational Systems is still well-known today for developing products to assist people with learning difficulties, and those who are blind or visually impaired, but other companies have become more involved with developing and improving speech software.[1]

The continuous speech recognition system became available in the first Dragon product in April of 1997. The computers required to run CSR easily cost $3500 at that time and were very primitive by today's standards. A large barrier to effective use of speech recognition was the lack of speed and accuracy due to low processing speeds and lack of RAM. This barrier, in addition to the high cost of hardware and inadequate headsets, made every day use of speech recognition a challenge.

---

[1]Intelligence, Automatic Speech Recognition (ASR) Speech /Voice Recognition, http://www.globalsecurity.org/intell/systems/asr.htm, Accessed September 20, 2010.

1.2 Improvements

The development of modern, high-speed PC processors in 2002 helped improve the speed and accuracy of speech recognition software. Both computer hardware and speech recognition software programs have had significant improvements over the past few years. Today, the average CPU is 1 GHz and has RAM levels of at least 1 GB making computers much more efficient. Many time-savings features have also been added to the software versions.

Originally, before the user could start dictating, they had to "train" the software by reading a series of passages that took about 45 minutes. Even after completing this initial training, the early versions were only about 75% accurate to begin with. Today, training the computer by reading passages takes less than 5 minutes and is optional. The out-of-the-box accuracy is about 95%.[2]

The average user can speak three times faster than they can type and can achieve remarkable accuracy at dictation speeds well over 100 words per minute with little effort. However, it does take time and patience at first to learn how to voice-write, edit, and format documents.
The time and effort you will spend in learning how to use speech recognition software effectively will save you a tremendous amount of time in the future and will increase your overall productivity. Think of all the things that you may compose on a daily basis: emails, reports, databases, spreadsheet data, press releases, minutes, articles, newsletters, books, dissertations, white papers, journals— you name it. Consider how much time you will save if you can produce these documents three times faster using voice-input instead of the keyboard.

Techno-journalist David Pogue had this to say about learning to use speech recognition software:
> *"But most people, alas, simply don't have the **patience**. There are so many times in life when an investment in time and learning up front leads to a long-term payoff. And in computing, that's especially true (learning to use macros in Word, learning a few keyboard shortcuts in Mac OS X, and so on). Dictation software falls squarely in that category. "For me, it's a lifesaver and very nearly magical — but only because I stuck with it. "*[3]

1.3 Learning a New Skill

Over the past several years, the expanded use of cell phones, mobile devices and the Internet has transformed us into a very text intensive society. Dictating, composing, and reading out loud are awkward for many people at first. Dictating or "voicing our thoughts" to a computer is different than writing or keying our thoughts. Before word processors were popular, most people would write everything on paper before they keyed it into the computer even when they could type faster than they could write. Now most people are comfortable in keying their thoughts directly into the computer without writing anything down first. It took time and practice to change our thought process and habits from "thinking and writing" to "thinking and keying/texting."It will also take time and practice to change our thought process from "thinking and keying/texting" to "thinking and dictating."

---

[2]Wood, Lamont, 15 July 2007 Special to LiveScience , "Speech Recognition Software Finally Works" http://www.livescience.com/technology/070716_speech_recognition.html, Accessed September 20, 2010
3(David Pogue, FROM THE DESK OF DAVIED POGUE: Learning to Talk to Your PC, New York Times, March 2004).

1.4 Current Uses for Speech Recognition

Speech recognition technology has advanced to the point where it is being used by more and more individuals in a wide variety of industries and professional careers every day. Most people can create documents using speech recognition software much faster than they can type. By learning to use speech as an alternate input method, students and professionals will increase their overall productivity and acquire a valuable skill that will give them a competitive edge as they advance in their education and careers. Because speech recognition software is being utilized by leading corporate, government, legal, criminal justice, education and medical organizations throughout the world, learning to use speech recognition effectively could increase employment opportunities.

1.5 Industries Currently Using Speech Recognition Technology

Healthcare

Dragon NaturallySpeaking is the most widely used speech recognition application in healthcare industry and is being used by a wide variety of healthcare workers including doctors, medical students, nurses, physician assistants, nurse practitioners, dentists, physical/occupational therapists, pharmacists, administrators, medical assistants, and other support staff. Hospitals rely on the technology to improve financial performance and raise the quality of care because physicians are able to dictate more detailed notes, in real time into the patient records system. This allows quicker access to the information by other clinicians and healthcare workers who provide the patient with care.

Currently, 21st Century technology offers physicians and health care providers a medical record paradigm that will not only vastly upgrade the process of producing, maintaining and safeguarding medical records but will, in a direct and fundamental way, actually improve the quality of medical care. The technology is Electronic Medical Records (EMRs).[3] The $19 billion dollars provided in the Federal Stimulus Bill has given a large incentive for health care to implement an EMR system and requires all medical facilities to upgrade to an EMR system by 2012. EMRs produce the most accurate and complete patient health record possible to date and help physicians share information and practice better medicine.

Although most of the current high-end Electronic Medical Record products have 'pick lists' or 'click and point' methodology to complete large portions of the patient medical record, the historical portion of the patient medical record typically has a great deal of information that cannot be easily foreseen by the developers and is text intensive. Therefore, speech input is more productive.

3Fisherman, Eric, Voice Recognition, 2005
http://www.voicerecognition.com/electronicmedicalrecord/emrvoice/
Accessed September 20, 2010.

Legal

Thousands of legal professionals incorporate speech recognition technology to dramatically reduce the time it takes to create everything from briefs and contracts to case documentation and correspondence. Law firms and legal departments deploy speech solutions broadly to speed document turnaround, reduce transcription costs, and streamline repetitive workflows – without having to change business processes or existing information systems. Each organization and even the individuals within each organization, use speech recognition for different purposes, based on their responsibilities, workflow, preferences, and other applications used. Speech recognition users include partners, associates, corporate counsel, judges, legal researchers, court reporters, law students, paralegals, mobile professionals, people with disabilities, transcriptionists, assistants, and other support staff.

Law Enforcement

Police departments use speech recognition to voice-enable patrol car computers to speed up the information collection and inquiry processes. Officers can dictate information an average of 68% faster than typing by hand. This enables the quick and safe completion of necessary paperwork and computer related tasks while on duty – providing additional time to focus on more important aspects of law enforcement, such as suppressing crime and patrolling the streets. It is used from uniformed patrol officers to the undercover vice detectives; from robbery/homicide investigators to school resource officers; from police service technicians to dispatchers and civilian support personnel.

Insurance

In today's insurance organizations, data entry often consumes the majority of a customer service representative's or agent's workday, limiting the amount of time they spend working on obtaining new clients for an agency. Using the keyboard to create reports and documentation is time-consuming, and organizations are plagued by high error rates, inconsistencies and slower processes. Speech recognition allows agents to document claims faster, more accurately and in a much more cost-effective manner. This allows the company to better manage heavy workloads, reduce overhead and provide better customer service.

Other Professions

Speech recognition is being used by many reporters, newspaper columnists, magazine editors, and authors. Careers such as closed caption, CART reporters for hearing-impaired individuals, and Internet streaming text providers, are also becoming more popular for voice inputting. The use of speech recognition technology will continue to increase as more and more industries learn the benefits and cost-effectiveness of this emerging inputting device.

Introducing speech recognition to students early in their academic development increases their ability to succeed during their secondary and post-secondary education, and it provides them with a valuable skill for future employment.

CHAPTER 2—GETTING STARTED

Before you can use speech recognition software effectively, you must create a user profile and adjust your microphone. Multiple users can be set up on the same computer system. When you add a user, a separate profile or folder is created that stores the individual user's unique voice files. This profile stores acoustic information about your voice that the software uses to recognize what you say and updates your own individual speech vocabulary as you add or customize, specialized words, names, acronyms, and abbreviations--thus, improving accuracy each time you use your voice profile.

2.1—Create Profile

Start Dragon NaturallySpeaking by clicking the **Dragon** icon  on your desktop or by choosing **Start, All Programs, Dragon NaturallySpeaking**.

The Profile Creation dialog box may open automatically. This would create your user profile in the default location on the computer's hard drive. Most users want to set up their profile to save in a specific location such as a network location or removable jump drive. Click **cancel** if you get this screen.

To set up your profile in a specific location, go to **Profile** on the Dragon Tool Bar and choose **New User Profile**, click **Browse** to choose location, and click **New**.

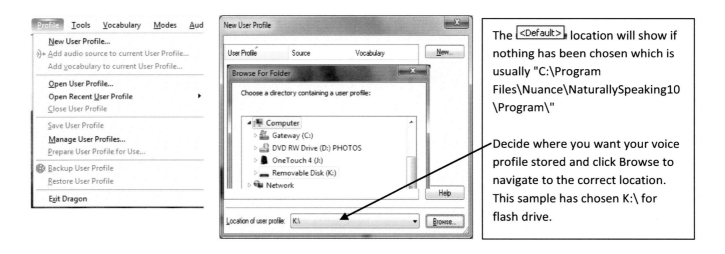

The <Default> location will show if nothing has been chosen which is usually "C:\Program Files\Nuance\NaturallySpeaking10\Program\"

Decide where you want your voice profile stored and click Browse to navigate to the correct location. This sample has chosen K:\ for flash drive.

Now you can follow the step-by-step wizard directions for creating a profile:

Click **Next** on the first screen and enter your first and last name. (User Profile names are case sensitive, so you cannot create names that are the same except for capitalization. For example, you cannot create both "Jean" and "jean". The following characters are also NOT allowed in User Profile names: / \ : * ? " < > | , =)

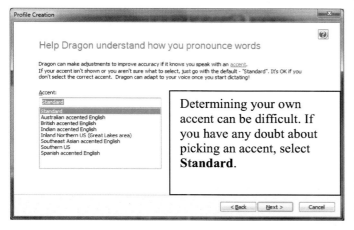

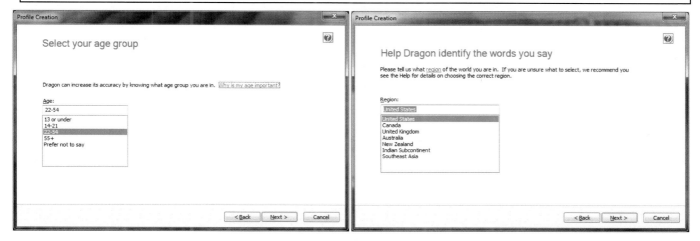

Determining your own accent can be difficult. If you have any doubt about picking an accent, select **Standard**.

You will get a chance to "Review your choices" on the next screen. Click back if you want to make any changes.

2.2 Check Microphone

Once your profile has been created, you will need to complete the steps for setting up your microphone. (You will also check your microphone on a daily basis by following these steps.)

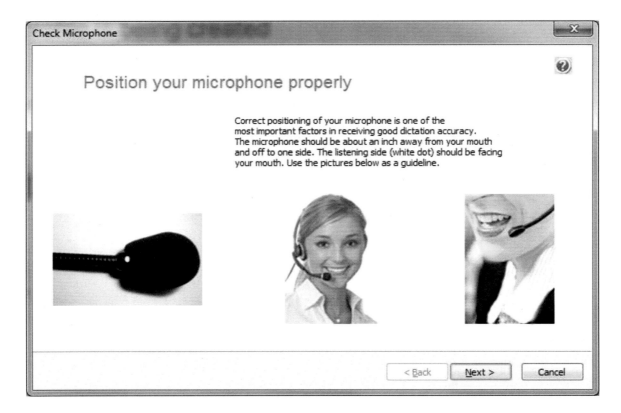

Once your microphone has been adjusted for proper placement, you will perform the volume check. When you are ready, click the "Start Volume Check" button and begin reading the material in the box in your normal voice. Do not say the punctuation. The blue slider will activate and move as it adjusts to your voice.

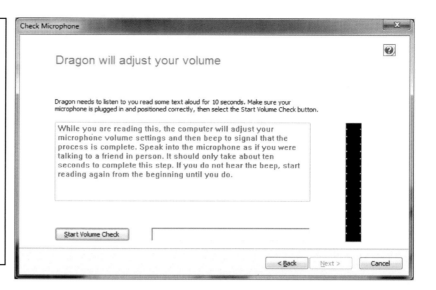

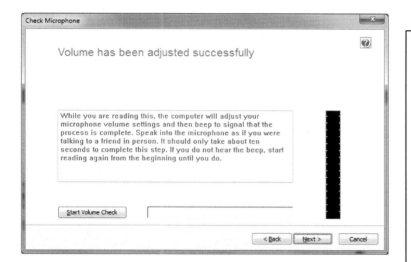

If you see "Volume has been adjusted successfully?" Click **next** to "Start Quality Check" and read the screen.

If you have passed the check, you will see Check Microphone: **Passed**.

If you get any error message saying your sound level is too high or too low…

Just click on OK and go on to quality check to see if microphone passes. If Microphone Check is "**poor**", Don't panic!

Check your headset connections and repeat the volume check & quality check until you get "Check Microphone: Passed".

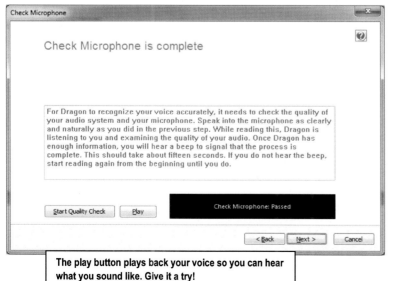

The play button plays back your voice so you can hear what you sound like. Give it a try!

2.3 General Training

When you are creating a profile for the first time, it is recommended that you choose the training option "show text with prompting." This will have you read for approximately four minutes so that Dragon can listen to you

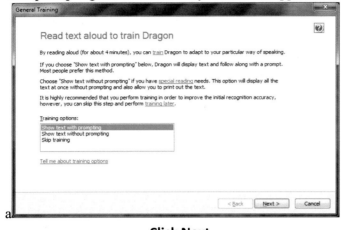 

a

Click Next **Click Next**

Select the first reading: What to Expect from Speech Recognition. Read all the training text screens and click OK when you're finished. You will see the adapting user profile message.

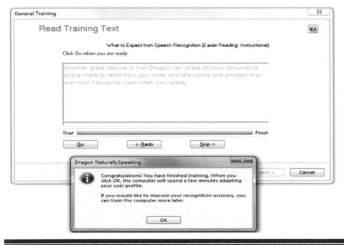 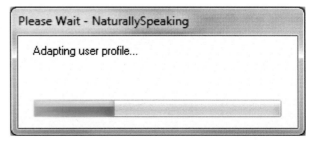

2.4 Profile Options

You will now see some screen choices for improving Dragon. These options will be utilized at a later time. Therefore, make the following selections as instructed under each dialog box below.

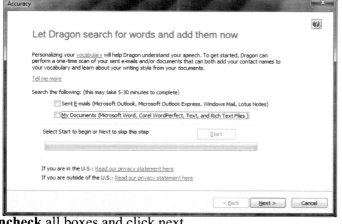

Uncheck all boxes and click next

Uncheck Automatically improve accuracy and click next

Choose **Don't** run Data Collection and click next

Click **Finish** on this screen.

The interactive tutorial may automatically open. If it does not open or you choose to close it, you can select it at another time by going to the Dragon Help menu.

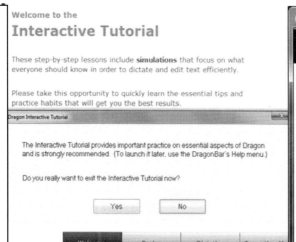

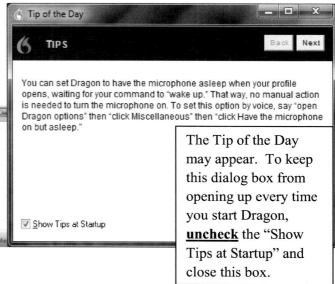

The Tip of the Day may appear. To keep this dialog box from opening up every time you start Dragon, **uncheck** the "Show Tips at Startup" and close this box.

You may receive the following message depending on your computer's processor and memory resources.

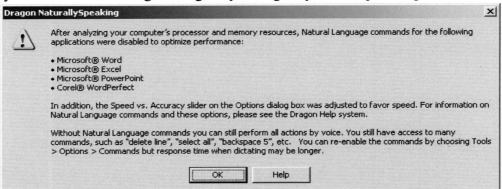

If this happens, you may want to click OK and then check the status and/or re-enable the Natural Language Commands by following the steps below.

2.5 Steps to Enable Natural Language Commands

1. On the DragonBar Choose •**Tools** •**Options**
2. Select the **Commands** Tab (*notice there are several items that are checked by default*)
3. Select **More Commands**
4. Select or de-select the programs you want enabled.
5. Click **OK**

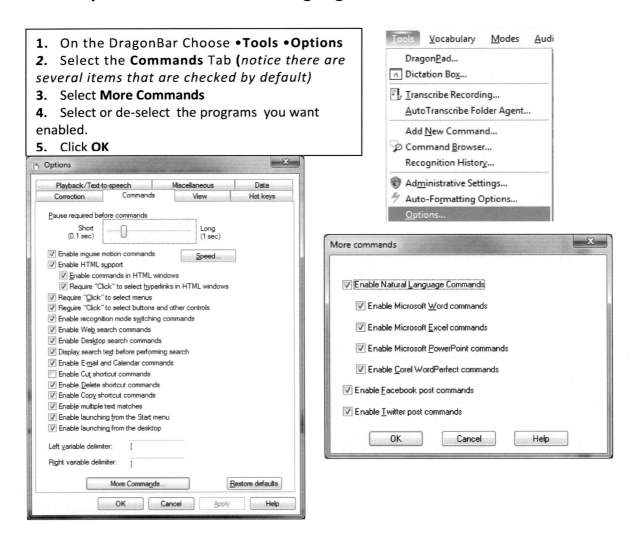

CHAPTER 3—GETTING READY TO DICTATE

Dragon NaturallySpeaking has an internal speech model that adapts to each individual voice through the training process. In Chapter 2, you created your own personal profile and completed the general training. This allows Dragon NaturallySpeaking™ to save the following important pieces of information for you every time you use the software:

- Audio settings
- Acoustic information gathered to learn user speech patterns
- Information about any words that have been trained
- User-generated vocabulary words or phrases
- Word usage information
- Settings changed in the Options dialog box
- Custom voice commands

In this chapter, you will become familiar with many of the components that will help you customize your profile further to increase your overall dictation recognition and accuracy.

3.1 Dragon Sidebar

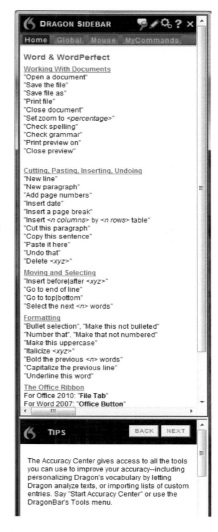

When you first open your profile, you should see the **Dragon Sidebar** on the right hand side of the screen. (*If the Sidebar is not displayed, go to DragonBar, Help and choose Dragon Sidebar*).

The Dragon Sidebar displays a selection of the most useful commands that the software recognizes for the current context, whether it is a particular program you are using or the Windows Desktop. The Sidebar is divided into upper and lower sections, called panes.

- The top pane of the Sidebar provides clickable links to online Help topics, shows examples of commands available in the current application, and organizes the information by tabs
- The lower pane of the Sidebar contains overall tips.

This can become a helpful resource as you become an experienced Dragon user. However, as a beginner, it is important to learn the basics before trying to memorize a lot of commands. **For now, hide the Dragon Sidebar by clicking the close box on the Sidebar.**

YOU WILL LEARN ABOUT USING COMMANDS AND THE SIDEBAR IN CHAPTER 7!

3.2 DragonBar

The **DragonBar** is designed to help you discover and quickly access important tools. In addition, it keeps important status indicators close together: Microphone status, Text Control indicator, Recognition Mode indicator, and messages from Dragon.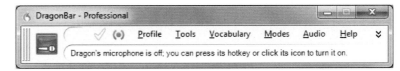

By default, the **DragonBar** is docked to the top of your screen.

Click on the Dragon icon to see a list of options for placement of your DragonBar.

This sample shows floating mode. You can choose your own individual preference.

You can also expand the **DragonBar** by clicking on the down chevron icon next to Help.

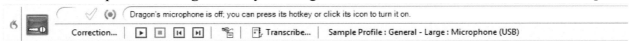

This is a good place to check to see if you have your own personal profile loaded. You should see your profile name where this one says "sample profile". You will also see additional shortcut icons that you will learn more about in future chapters. **Click the up chevron ⌃ again to hide these extra options.**

The DragonBar also contains menus that are specific to the Dragon program.

- The "**Profile**" menu includes items that are used to create, edit and manage your personal profile.
- The "**Tools**" menu allows you to change your options, work with recordings, and add commands.
- The "**Vocabulary**" menu allows you to add words and phrases, train words and manage vocabulary.
- The "**Modes**" menu allows you to switch between dictation modes. (*The Normal Mode is most common and is what you should use. (You will have a chance to experiment with the different modes in future exercises.*)
- The "**Audio**" menu allows you to check your microphone, play or read back text and improve accuracy.
- The "**Help**" menu provides many useful Dragon tips for a variety of topics.

3.3 Formatting Options

There are several formatting features preset in Dragon NaturallySpeaking. However, you can customize the default settings by choosing or saying **Switch to DragonBar, Tools**, **Auto-Formatting Options** and deselect or select the choices you want.

Note: DragonNaturally Speaking inserts one space after a period by default. Many instructors still like two spaces. There is also an option for automatically adding commas and periods. However, it is **NOT** recommended to choose this option unless you are an experienced Dragon user with strong dictation skills. **Keeping the default settings is recommended**. For more information on these options, you can click the Help button.

3.4 Reduce Size of Profiles

As you make corrections and perform additional training, Dragon stores this data as .dra files in an archive to use with Acoustic Optimizer. In the professional version, these speech files can also be stored with dictated documents. Storing these files causes the speech profile to grow quite large (200-300 MB) in a short period of time. Storing these large profiles can become problematic for schools or organizations with limited remote storage space. On the **DragonBar** you can click or say **Tools**, **Options**, **Data**

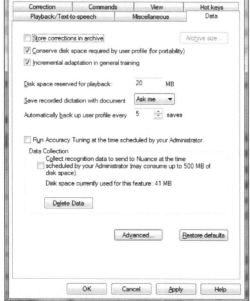

To reduce the size of the student profile:

1. Uncheck **"Store corrections in archive.**
2. Uncheck **"Data Collection"**
3. Check **"Conserve disk space required by user profile"**
4. Check **"Incremental adaptation of additional training"**
5. **"Disk space reserved for playback"** default is 100 MB. *This can be lowered--in this sample it was lowered to 20.*
6. The Ask me option is on by default for:

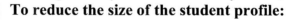

The **"ask me"** option gives you this dialogue box every time you go to save a document. Many users do not use this feature, and choose to **Never.**

3.5 Changing Hot Keys Options

You learned that you can turn the microphone on and off by pressing the numeric + key on the standard numeric keypad. This is known as a "Hot Key" or keyboard shortcut. Many of the keys on the standard numeric keypad are set as a default Hot Key for Dragon. Hot Keys are very beneficial and can save you time. However, not all computer keyboards have a standard numeric keypad or if you want to use your numeric keypad while Dragon is activated you will want to change the default Hot Key settings

1. Go to the DragonBar Choose •**Tools** •**Options**
2. Click on the **Hot keys** tab
3. Notice the **Options Box 1** below shows the default Hot keys listed in { } next to the desired command. (NumKey stands for numeric keyboard).

Options Box 1

To Change the Hot keys:
1. Click on desired command box…example Microphone on/off.
2. **Set Hot Key** box will appear.
3. Press the key(s) on the keyboard that you want to use for the desired Hot key*.
4. Click **OK**.

(*It is recommended to use 2 keys together that are not used for other features when setting a Hot key). **Option Box 2** shows an example of changing the Microphone on /off to{alt and /} keys. You would press the Alt and slash keys at the exact same time to activate this shortcut.

Options box 2

It is up to you if you want to keep the default Hot key settings or change them. In the sample below, **Options Box 3** shows changes for **Microphone on/off, Correction, DragonBar menu** and **Microphone sleep/on.**

Options Box 3

Alt / (slash) is **Microphone on/off** instead of the **+** on numeric keypad

Alt . (period) is **Correction** instead of **−** on numeric keypad

Alt , (comma) is **DragonBar Menu** instead of the ***** on the numeric keypad

Alt ' (apostrophe) is **Microphone sleep/on** instead of the **/** on the numeric keypad

Determine if you want to use Hot keys and if you would like to change any of the defaults settings by following the steps on the previous page.

3.6 Microphone Tips

The position and tuning of your microphone is very important. Start by keeping the tip of the microphone about 3/4 of an inch away from your lower lip, and, if possible, move it slightly to the side so it is not directly in front of your mouth. This helps avoid breathing errors.

1) Avoid touching or holding the microphone tip—the part of the microphone you speak into.

2) Move the microphone tip slightly further away from your mouth if extra words appear on the screen caused by your breathing.

3) Keep your chin slightly elevated when you speak, as if you are talking to a person. Don't talk down into your chest.

4) Retest your headset if you notice a sudden drop in accuracy or performance or if you can't seem to control breathing errors, by saying • **CHECK AUDIO** or choosing **Audio, Check Microphone** from the DragonBar Menu.

5) Retest your headset if your acoustic environment changes. This is true if the environment gets much louder or quieter than normal.

6) Test the headset. If audio problems persist, try plugging the headset into different port or try using a different headset (analog and/or USB). If the problem continues, try using the headset on a different computer. Audio problems may be the result of a defective headset or a sound card issue.

7) Don't forget to turn off the microphone when you are done speaking.

3.7 Microphone Commands

Beginners with speech recognition stumble because they simply do not control the microphone. Turning the microphone on and off is as simple as:

- Clicking or tapping the Dragon microphone icon on the DragonBar/Task Bar with a mouse or digital pen
- Pressing the numeric + key on the number pad of an extended keyboard (or other designated "hot key", see Hot Key Options on page 17-18)
- Saying MICROPHONE OFF

The microphone needs to be turned off/or hibernated when NOT dictating.

Unlike a passive keyboard, which is waiting to be pressed into action, the microphone is an active device. It is best to turn the **microphone off** when not speaking to your computer. However, you may also put the microphone in **hibernation** mode by saying **STOP LISTENING** or **GO TO SLEEP**. When the microphone is in hibernation mode, it is actually still ON and is waiting for a voice command. Some people have problems with the microphone turning itself back on before they are ready. Therefore, it is recommended the microphone be turned off verses hibernating.

The following exercises gives you practice with using Microphone Commands.

3.8 Microphone Activation Commands

1. The DragonBar shows the status of the microphone and provides messages. Turn the microphone on by clicking or tapping on the red **Microphone** button next to the DragonBar Icon.

2. The Microphone will pop up. Remain quiet and watch the microphone volume meter. It will remain yellow when you are quiet. It will turn green or even red as you speak.

3. Turn the microphone completely off by pressing the **+ key**. You can turn your microphone back on again by clicking it with your mouse or by pressing the + key on your numeric keypad. Press the **+ key** to turn the microphone on.

4. Say • **MICROPHONE OFF.** This command turns your microphone completely off.

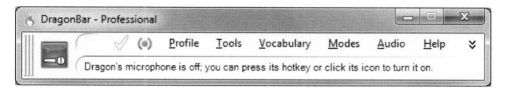

3.9 Microphone Hibernation Commands

The dot (•) reminds you to be silent for 1/2 second before saying a command.
Hibernating your microphone puts the microphone in a pause mode so you can talk to others and then reactivate the microphone by voice. (Try the following)

1. Turn on the microphone by clicking the icon. Say • **STOP LISTENING.**

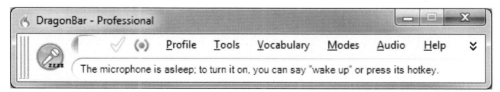

2. To wake your microphone from hibernation, say • **LISTEN TO ME.**

3. Use other commands to turn the microphone on and off. Say • **GO TO SLEEP and WAKE UP.** (Be sure to turn microphone off before going to next page)

3.10 Opening Dragon Menus by Voice

The **DragonBar** contains menus that are specific to the Dragon program. You can select any menu item by voice by saying "**Switch to DragonBar**" to make the DragonBar active and say the name of the menu.

1. Be sure Dragon NaturallySpeaking is open and the DragonBar is visible. (All other applications should be closed.) Turn the microphone on by clicking or tapping the **Microphone** button or by pressing the **+ key.**

2. Say • **SWITCH TO DRAGONBAR** to select the DragonBar. Say "Profile" and notice the item list appears. Say • **CANCEL** to close the Profile menu.

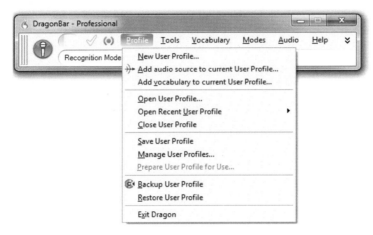

3. Say • **TOOLS** to open the Tools menu. Say • **CANCEL** to close the Tools menu.

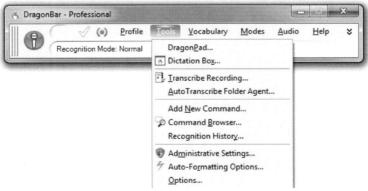

4. Say • **VOCABULARY** to open the Vocabulary menu. Say • **CANCEL** to close the menu.

5. Say • **MODES** to open the Modes menu. Say • **CANCEL** to close the menu.

6. Say • **AUDIO** to open the Audio menu. Say • **CANCEL** to close the menu.

7. Say• **HELP** to open the Help menu. Say • **CANCEL** to close the menu.

You will learn more about these menu options as you work through more exercises.

3.11 Start Programs by Voice

You can easily open programs by voice by either saying "open" or "start" and the name of the program you would like to open.

1. Open Microsoft Word by saying either:

    - **START MICROSOFT WORD** or • **OPEN MICROSOFT WORD**

2. Close Microsoft Word using voice commands. Say either:
    - **CLICK CLOSE** or **CLOSE DOCUMENT**
    If you are prompted to save, say • **NO.**

3. Open Microsoft Excel by saying:
    - **START MICROSOFT EXCEL** or **OPEN MICROSOFT EXCEL**

4. Close Microsoft Excel using voice commands. If prompted to save, say • **NO.**

5. Try opening and closing other programs with such commands as • **START INTERNET EXPLORER,** • **OPEN NOTEPAD** or • **START PAINT.** If these programs are in your Start menu, they will open.

6. Close any open programs by saying either • **CLICK CLOSE, CLOSE DOCUMENT** or by saying • **FILE, EXIT** or **OFFICE BUTTON, EXIT** then say • **MICROPHONE OFF** to turn off your mic.

3.12 Dictation Box

Normally you can dictate and use Dragon NaturallySpeaking voice commands in any window. However, you may occasionally find an application or a specific window where some voice commands won't work or will not work consistently. In these instances, **Dragon may automatically open the Dictation Box.** This is a special window that allows the user to dictate, edit, and use basic commands and then transfer text to the desired program. The **Dictation Box** can be opened by saying: **SHOW DICTATION BOX** (or by clicking Tools, Dictation Box on the DragonBar).

You will have the opportunity to use the Dictation Box in future exercises. For now, try the following example to practice commands.

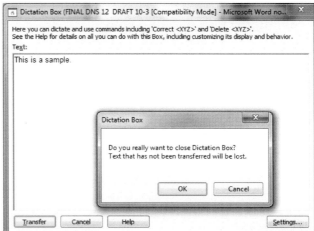

> **Example**
> - Say **Show Dictation Box** (*the dictation box should open in a few seconds*).
> - Dictate: **This is a sample** (*you should see the words appear in the window--don't worry about mistakes*).
> - Say **Click Cancel** (*normally you would say click transfer and text would go into selected application*)
> - *Say* **Click OK** (*this will close the Dictation Box*).

Remember you do not need to do everything hands-free. Use whatever device is most productive for you. If it is faster or easier for you to use your keyboard or mouse to open or close programs that is okay. These lessons are designed to help familiarize you with speech recognition software options and commands.

3.13 Properly Exiting Dragon NaturallySpeaking

Dragon NaturallySpeaking actually learns how you speak and compensates for misrecognitions and your regional accent as you use the software. In the practice exercises in later chapters, you will start correcting errors using specialized Dragon NaturallySpeaking techniques. These techniques will improve your recognition accuracy well beyond anything you can do with enunciation alone.

You must exit and save properly in order to save all of the improvements you have made to your user file. If you correct mistakes and do not save properly, Dragon NaturallySpeaking will forget all of the improvements to your user file's accuracy.

Say "Switch to DragonBar," "Profile" or Click Profile, Say or Click "Save user Profile", Say or Click "Exit Dragon". Click "NO" when asked if you want to save recorded audio.

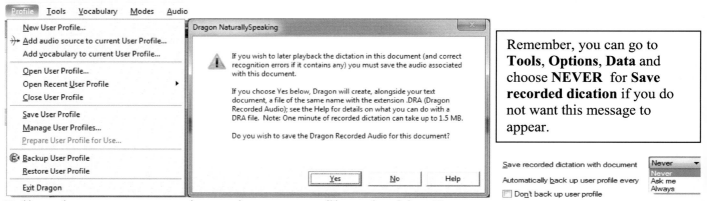

Remember, you can go to **Tools**, **Options**, **Data** and choose **NEVER** for **Save recorded dication** if you do not want this message to appear.

Follow these steps to practice saving your profile and exiting Dragon.

3.14 Opening Dragon NaturallySpeaking

Follow these steps to Open your User Profile, Check Audio and Turn Off your Microphone.

Click on the Dragon Icon or go to Start, Programs and choose Dragon NaturallySpeaking. The Open User Profile dialog box will appear: Click your name and Click Open. *If you do not see your name, Click Browse to the location you saved your User Profile.*

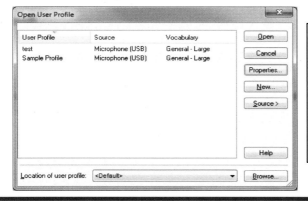

Remember the first thing you should do after opening your profile is tune your microphone by saying **Check Audio**.

(You can also Click on the **Audio** menu and choose **Check Microphone**.

3.15 Microsoft Office Tips

This training manual is designed to work with various versions of Microsoft Office including 2003, 2007 and 2010. Most Dragon commands work the same for all programs. However, Office 2007 has the Office button vs. the File menu.

1. **To access the Office Button** (similar to the "File" menu in previous versions) by voice, say **"Office Button" or "Click Office Button." The file menu will open with the familiar choices of Save, Save As, Open, Print, etc.** Remember – most of the natural commands used in Word XP or Word 2003 are the same for Word 2007 and 2010
   Examples:
   - New Document
   - Save (or Save Document)
   - Save As (or Save Document As)
   - Open Document (or Open File)
   - Click Close (or Close Document)
   - Print Document

2. **To Access Word 2007 Ribbon Menu Items**

   - To access titles on the Word 2007 or 2010 menu ribbon, simply dictate the title and all subsequent titles. For example:
   - Page Layout, Margins, Narrow
   - Insert • Table • Insert Table (automatically goes to first box) Numeral 3 • Tab • Numeral 10 (However, it is still easier to just say "Insert a 3 by 10 Table.")

   - **Tip**: Run your mouse over the icons on the Word 2007/2010 menu ribbon to see the icon titles. Select the icon by voice by saying the icon title. Examples:
     — Show Paragraph Marks (or Hide Paragraph Marks)
     — Bullets, Numbering, Bold, Underline
     — Grow Font (or Shrink Font)

   - Some drop down menus (such as text highlight color) must be expanded by using the mouse to click the down arrow. After drop down list is expanded, user may move around by using directional commands, such as move down 2, move right 3, and they say mouse click to select the highlighted choice.

   - Some users prefer to use the mouse to click menu options instead of using voice commands.

   - If the software does not recognize an item in a menu list, try using navigational commands (move right one, move down 2, press enter, etc.).

CHAPTER 4—DICTATION BASICS

When first starting to use speech recognition software, many people find it easier to read something to the computer instead of composing or dictating from scratch. The more you talk to your computer in your natural speaking voice the better the software will recognize your unique speech patterns and dialect.

Talking to your computer may seem awkward at first. You are learning a new skill; it takes time to practice and learn the basics. Follow the dictation tips and complete the step-by-step activities in this chapter to become more comfortable with dictating.

4.1 Dictating Tips

- Do NOT watch your screen as you dictate and do NOT try to correct your errors as you speak. Say what you're going to say, and don't worry about misrecognized words or mistakes. (You'll learn how to correct these later.)

- Speak naturally at your normal speed. Pronounce each word clearly, not loudly, and in a way that is comfortable for you.

- Say each word ending clearly. For example, **and say something** not **ansay somethin'**.

- Do not speak too deliberately! Keep words together. Do not speak in syllables. For example, say **conversations.** Do not say, **con verse say shuns.** If you find yourself breaking words into syllables, slightly pick up the pace of your speaking.

- For best recognition, speak in longer phrases rather than short phrases or individual words. This helps with fluency and allows Dragon to run a grammar/statistical check of your sentences, thereby improving accuracy.

- Dictate all punctuation marks.

Have patience and think of ways that you can practice talking to your computer:

The more you practice talking to your computer, the more comfortable you will become and the more naturally you will speak. You can practice a little each day by reading something out loud to the computer.

Think about some things you may be planning to read over the next few days. For example, if you are going to read a newspaper article, instead of reading it silently to yourself, activate your speech recognition software and read the article out loud into Microsoft Word or another text application.

Practicing tips: Don't think about reading to your computer. Just read the article without looking at your screen or worrying about mistakes or unique words. It is okay if you stumble over words or the computer doesn't understand everything you say. You are practicing talking out loud to your computer and the speech recognition software is recording how you speak to improve your overall recognition and accuracy.

4.2 Practice Dictating, Selecting and Deleting Text

Say punctuation marks like • PERIOD.

1. Turn on your Microphone. Say •**Start Microsoft Word**

2. After your program opens, dictate the following (do not pay attention to errors or try to make corrections):

   Using speech recognition is fun PERIOD Dragon NaturallySpeaking is easy to learn PERIOD Start by speaking in simple sentences PERIOD Remember to say punctuation PERIOD Dragon wants you to speak naturally PERIOD Do not stop between words or break words into syllables PERIOD Speak to your computer the way television news personalities read the news PERIOD

3. Press the + **key** on your numeric keypad to turn off your microphone.

4. Count your mistakes. If you made five or less errors, you have achieved 90 percent accuracy or better.

5. Press the + **key** on your numeric keypad.

6. Say • **SELECT ALL** to select all of the text.

7. Say • **BACKSPACE** to delete the highlighted text.

8. For practice, repeat the dialogue again. Say • **PERIOD** as needed.

   Using speech recognition is fun. Dragon NaturallySpeaking is easy to learn. Start by speaking in simple sentences. Remember to say punctuation. Dragon wants you to speak naturally. Do not stop between words or break words into syllables. Speak to your computer the way television news personalities read the news.

9. Press the + **key** on your numeric keypad to turn your microphone OFF.

10. Count your mistakes. With 5 errors or less, you are over 90 percent accurate.

11. Press the + **key** on your numeric keypad to turn your microphone ON.

12. Say • **CLEAR DOCUMENT, or** • **CLEAR PAGE** to delete the text..

13. Exit Word by saying • **CLICK CLOSE** or **CLOSE DOCUMENT. Hint**: (In Office 2007, Click **CLOSE** may not work but **CLOSE DOCUMENT** will).

14. Say **Click NO** (*don't save*) • **MICROPHONE OFF.**

Use the • **NEW LINE** command when you need to make a line break. This is the same as pressing the Enter Key once. Use the • **NEW PARAGRAPH** command to create a double space, this is like pressing the Enter Key twice.

Tip: When dictating, say these commands sharply after a • 1/2 second of complete silence.

- **NEW LINE**   not   • **NEW LiiyNE**
- **NEW PARAGRAPH** not   • **NEW PARAGRaa**

    If you have trouble with these commands, you can say PRESS ENTER or press your Enter key on the keyboard. (You will learn how to train hard-to-recognize commands in Chapter 6).

Speech recognition software also allows you to say our punctuation marks and place them exactly where you want them to go. Look at the following examples:

- ■ Say • **COMMA for** ,
- ■ Say • **EXCLAMATION MARK** or • **EXCLAMATION POINT for** !
- ■ Say • **COLON for** :
- ■ Say • **SEMICOLON for** ;

4.3   Practice New Paragraph & New Line

While practicing the • NEW LINE and • NEW PARAGRAPH commands, do not be too concerned about correcting your dictation errors. You'll learn to make corrections later!

1.   Turn on your microphone if it is off. If you have closed Microsoft Word, open the program once again.

2.   Speak the following dialogue. Remember to say punctuation marks and pause a second or two (•) before saying commands. *If you make a few mistakes, ignore them for this exercise:* *

Wow! I get to go on a trip to Australia. • NEW PARAGRAPH

The Australian outback is full of animals. • NEW PARAGRAPH
The animals include: (NEW LINE)
kangaroos (NEW LINE)
crocodiles (NEW LINE)
snakes (NEW PARAGRAPH)

Kangaroos live in the Australian outback. (NEW LINE)
crocodiles live in the swamp. (NEW LINE)
snakes live in the trees. (NEW LINE)

*Notice if you say a punctuation mark at the end of the sentence or say NEW PARAGRAPH, the next word is automatically capitalized. If you say NEW LINE, without a punctuation mark at the end of the line, the next word will not be capitalized – the software considers the new line to be a continuation of the same sentence. Look at animal list above.

3.   Say "**Click Close**" and "**Click NO**" to close Microsoft Word without saving.

4.4 Practice Dictating—Speak Clearly & Use Commands

1. Turn on your Microphone. Say •**Start Microsoft Word**

2. After your program opens, dictate the following two paragraphs saying all punctuation marks and New Paragraph command. (Do not pay attention to errors or try to make corrections):

   We are learning how to dictate using speech recognition software. This software allows us to use our voice in addition to the keyboard or mouse to create documents. The computer will type what we dictate or do what we command as we dictate words, numbers, symbols and a variety of formatting commands. (*NEW PARAGRAPH*)

   We will learn what commands to use and how to train the computer to recognize our unique voices by completing exercises in this training manual. Once we have learned some basics, we will use the speech recognition software to create many different documents including emails, letters, reports, and spreadsheets.

3. Press the **+ key** on your numeric keypad to **turn off** your microphone.

4. Count your mistakes. There are 100 words in these two paragraphs. To figure your accuracy percentage, subtract the number of errors from the total words to get the number of correct words (net). Divide the net words by the total words. Example: If you had five errors, your net words would be 95. Divide 95 by 100 and you get 95 or 95% accuracy. Remember, your accuracy levels will improve the more you use the software.

4.5 Read Text to Improve Accuracy

You most likely speak between 110 and 180 words per minute. Everyone has their own natural speaking speed. Remember, **accuracy** is more important than speed. If you try to talk much faster or much slower than you normally speak your accuracy will be lower.

As mentioned at the beginning of this chapter, one of the best ways to improve your speech recognition accuracy is to practice reading out loud to the computer. Dragon NaturallySpeaking has additional built-in stories that you can read to help improve your overall accuracy. Most people do not need to read more than one of these stories. However, if your accuracy is not continuously improving over time, you may want to read additional text passages by following the steps below:

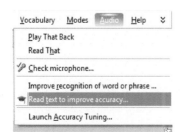 Go to the **Audio Menu** on the **DragonBar** and **choose Read Text to Improve Accuracy.** (You can also do this by voice by saying "Switch to DragonBar", "Audio", "Read Text to Improve Accuracy")

Follow the General Training Steps:

 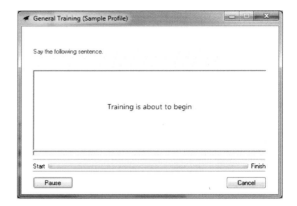

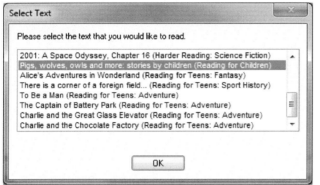

You can choose **any** of these text passages. **Note:** There are passages designed specifically for teens. The passage "Pigs, wolves, owls and more" is recommended for lower level readers.

You don't need to completely finish text. If you are running out of time, you can cut off the reading by choosing **Finish** followed by **OK.** The amount you have been able to read will be processed. You can always come back and read more at a later time.

Click Yes

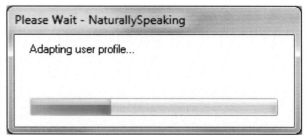

When using a file server, this process may take longer. For classrooms, you may want to limit the number of students that are adapting their profile at the same time.

CHAPTER 5—SELECTING, CORRECTING, SAVING, SPELLING

Remember, when you are first learning to use speech recognition software, it is important to follow the proper dictating tips and practice dictating without worrying about any mistakes. Not only will you become more comfortable in talking to the computer, the software will actually learn how you speak and compensate for mispronunciations and your regional accent.

Besides reading additional text, there are several things that you can do to help increase the overall accuracy of your speech profile. In the practice exercises ahead, you will start using specialized Dragon NaturallySpeaking techniques such as correcting errors and training misrecognized words. These techniques will improve your recognition accuracy well beyond anything you could do with enunciation alone.

5.1 Selecting Words by Voice

To make corrections, you will often need to select the text first. You could select the text with your mouse or keyboard. However, it is more efficient to use the **SELECT** command.

The voice command to select a word or phrase is SELECT <text> *(<text> is the word or phrase you want to select)* or you can say SELECT <text> THROUGH <text> to select a word or phrase at the beginning and at the end of the range you want to select.

Open Microsoft Word: Dictate the following sentences and follow the instructions to select a specific word or phrase:

George Washington was the first president of the United States.

Remember the moment of silence (•) before you say the • **SELECT** command. However, DO NOT hesitate after you say the • **SELECT** command. For example:

- ■   Say • **SELECT George Washington**
- ■   Don't say ... **SELECT** hesitate **George Washington**

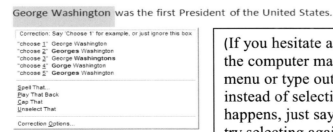

(If you hesitate after the word select, the computer may choose the select menu or type out the word "select" instead of selecting text. If this happens, just say "**unselect that**" and try selecting again without hesitating.)

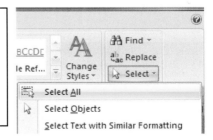

SELECT ALL, **BACK SPACE** and then **dictate** this sentence:

James went to the University to get an education. He went to class almost every day. After school he went to work. There was very little time to play.

Say "**SELECT**" <to>

James went to the University to get an education. He went to class almost every day. After school he went to work. There was very little time to play.

Notice each occurrence of the word "to" is numbered. To select a specific occurrence say Choose <#>. For example, Choose **4**.

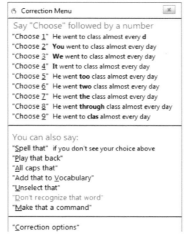

Notice the quick correction list will display words that are homonyms or close to the sound of the word "to". You will learn more about this correction box later. For now, get used to its presence as you practice selecting words.

Say "**UNSELECT THAT**" (notice correction box goes away and isn't selected)

Say "**SELECT**" <He> THROUGH <day>

James went to the University to get an education. He went to class almost every day. After school he went to work. There was very little time to play.

This is a quick way to select a phrase or larger amounts of text

---

5.2 Select Multiple Text

You can **SELECT** individual words, lines, paragraphs, or even pages. For now, let's keep it simple and just look at lines, sentences, and paragraphs.

Here are the new commands we will be working with:
- **SELECT LINE**
- **SELECT SENTENCE**
- **SELECT PARAGRAPH**

Dictate the following paragraph. (Again, don't worry about any mistakes. You will just be practicing the **SELECT** command).

Using speech recognition is fun. Dragon NaturallySpeaking is easy to learn. Start by speaking in simple sentences. Remember to say punctuation. Dragon wants you to speak naturally. Do not stop between words or break words into syllables. Speak to your computer the way television news personalities read the news.

SELECT "fun"

Using·speech·recognition·is·fun.·Dragon·NaturallySpeaking·is·easy·to·learn.·Start·by·speaking·in·simple·

SELECT "sentence"

Using·speech·recognition·is·fun.·Dragon·NaturallySpeaking·is·easy·to·learn.·Start·by·speaking·in·simple·

SELECT "line"

Using·speech·recognition·is·fun.·Dragon·NaturallySpeaking·is·easy·to·learn.·Start·by·speaking·in·simple·
sentences.·Remember·to·say·punctuation.· select line n·wants·you·to·speak·naturally.·Do·not·stop·between·

SELECT "paragraph"

Using·speech·recognition·is·fun.·Dragon·NaturallySpeaking·is·easy·to·learn.·Start·by·speaking·in·simple·
sentences.·Remember·to·say·punctuation.·Dragon·wants·you·to·speak·naturally.·Do·not·stop·between·
words·or·break·words·into· select paragraph peak·to·your·computer·the·way·television·news·personalities·
read·the·news.¶

Practice the SELECT command by selecting any words, phrases, lines, or sentences on your own.

Notes:

- You can cancel a selection by saying **UNSELECT THAT** selecting different text, or moving the insertion point to another part of the document.

- In most instances, the "select" command will display a number next to each instance of the word, allowing you to select all instances or just a specific instance.

- If you are dictating into an application that happens **not** to display a number next to each instance of the word, you need to use the **SELECT AGAIN** command. This commands searches for the next instance of the same word throughout the text.

5.3 Correcting Using the Correction Box or Select and Say

A misrecognition occurs when Dragon NaturallySpeaking almost, but not quite, guesses the correct word. As you **SELECT** any word or phrase, the top alternatives will appear in the Quick Correct list. More often than not, when Dragon does make a mistake, the correct word or phrase will be in the Quick Correct list. Choose the correct alternative from the list with the **CHOOSE <number>** command, as in **CHOOSE 1,** or **CHOOSE 4.** If the correct alternative is not on the list, use the **SELECT and SAY** command. This is when you select the incorrect word or phrase and say the correct word or phrase again.

Speech recognition is a phrase technology. If you speak in phrases, the software will calculate the probability of certain word combinations appearing together. This feature can reconcile most homonym situations such as, "Mr. Wright will write the right instructions today." If you correct phrases, the software mathematically calculates how frequently certain combinations of words appear together. When you correct words with the **SELECT and SAY** or **CHOOSE** options, Dragon remembers and the probability of missing the same word again in the same context diminishes drastically. The correction box is one of the fastest ways to improve your accuracy.

Steps for Correcting with Choose command:

A.   Use the • **SELECT <text>** command to choose misrecognized words or phrases.

> **Puzzled?** *Why is Dragon not selecting my misrecognitions?* Don't pause between the command word SELECT and the misrecognition. For example, say • **SELECT PROBLEM,** not • **SELECT <hesitate> PROBLEM.**

> **Puzzled?** *What if I have lots of trouble voice-selecting my misrecognitions?* Select the word with your mouse or digital pen and press the minus (-) key or say • **CORRECT THAT.** The correction box window will open.

B.   If the correct word appears in the Correction window, say • **CHOOSE 1,** or • **CHOOSE 2,** or • **CHOOSE 3,** etc., to correct the error.

C.   If the correct option does not appear in the Correction window, try saying the word or phrase again more clearly. This is known as **SELECT and SAY**.

D.   After two attempts, fix the error with the keyboard and move on. You will learn to fix these pesky errors in later exercises.

Example:

> o   **Voice-writing requires practice, and lots of it. People at just the pace of their writing to the efficiency of their input tools. In centuries past, writers would saddle their thoughts and slow them down to a walk when crafting paragraphs with paper and pencil.**

(The words *at just* appeared instead of *adjust.* The correction was made simply by saying • **SELECT at just, CHOOSE 1**).

Dictate the example paragraph above yourself and use the Select and Choose commands to make any corrections.

5.4 Practice Dictating, Selecting, and Choosing

Dictate the following paragraphs and practice using the "Steps for Correcting with Choose Command" that you learned in Exercise 5.3. Remember to dictate the entire paragraph before selecting and correcting any of the mistakes. DO NOT try to correct as you dictate.

1. Turn on your microphone. Open Microsoft Word with your voice. Say • **NEW DOCUMENT** to open a blank Word page.

2. Say the following dialogue:

   People have the ability to carry on conversations and tell stories. Almost everyone can relate to a story and say something meaningful. Today they have the software to convert their speech into typed text.

3. Correct any mistakes using the **SELECT** <text> and **CHOOSE** or **SELECT and SAY** commands. (Review the steps in the previous exercise if necessary).

4. Keep this paragraph on your page.

5. Say "NEW PARAGRAPH"

6. Now try this more complex paragraph. Be sure to say the hyphen between the words *voice* and *writing* in the following way: *voice hyphen writing. (Pre-reading the paragraph in your mind before speaking will help you smooth out the rough spots in your mind before you start to speak.)*

   Voice-writing requires practice and lots of it. People adjust the pace of their writing to the efficiency of their input tools. In centuries past, writers would saddle their thoughts and slow them down to a walk when crafting paragraphs with paper and pencil.

7. Again, select and correct any mistakes using the SELECT and CHOOSE commands.

8. Say "NEW PARAGRAPH"

9. Dictate the following nine sentences and use same • **CHOOSE** technique to correct errors (*Label this section by saying "**Sentences**": use the • NEW PARAGRAPH command after each sentence to separate each sentence with a double space."*)

Sentences:

He wants to go to the Olympics once in his life.

Mr. Wright will write the right instructions on the assignment.

They are on their way there.

To improve your accuracy, always correct every mistake you make.

Don't leave errors up in the air!

I have already checked, and they are all ready.

May I advise you on the advice you are giving to others?

I don't know whether you have noticed, but the weather is awful today.

He threw the ball through the target.

(You will save these paragraphs and sentences by following the steps on the next page.)

5.5 Saving Documents

There are several ways that you can use voice commands to save documents. However, the easiest commands are "Save Document" or "Save Document AS"

Say "**Save Document AS**"

If you are using the professional version of Dragon NaturallySpeaking, you may get the following message.

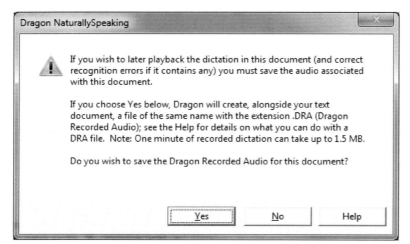

This feature is used mainly in medical and legal offices. However, recorded voice files take lots of memory from your hard drive. Normally you will select **NO** to save the space on your computer's drive.

Click **NO**-- the Save As dialog box will appear.

Use your mouse to navigate to the location where you would like to save your file. *In this example, a folder was created in My Documents called Dragon Exercises.*

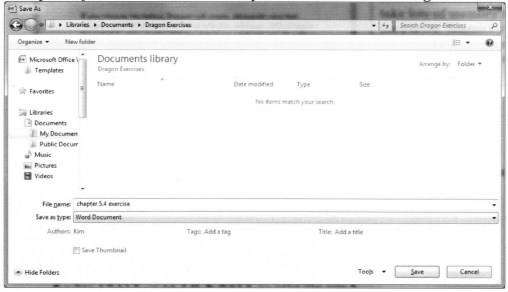

With the cursor in the Filename box, you can use your voice to name your document. Say "**chapter 5 point 5 exercise**"

Say **CLICK SAVE** to save the file. **Clear Document**.

5.6 Quick Correction Commands

Most of the time it is best to dictate then go back and make corrections. However, there are some quick correction commands that you can use if you know that you have misspoken or wish to erase the last phrase or phrases you have spoken. These commands include:

• **DELETE THAT** – erases "selected" text

• **SCRATCH THAT** – erases the last spoken words after the last pause

• **CANCEL THAT** – works like SCRATCH THAT, but it will also "undo" spoken commands. This may be the most efficient command to use for quick corrections.

• **UNDO THAT** – will undo the last command or action; repeating this command is like hitting the Redo button in Microsoft Word

• **RESUME WITH** -- allows you to erase text back to the indicated location. This is useful when you are composing and change your thoughts.

Open a New Document and dictate the following paragraph and practice the • **DELETE THAT,** • **SCRATCH THAT,** • **UNDO THAT** and • **CANCEL THAT** commands.

> **Speech recognition is better than I imagined. I can now type as fast as I can talk. I know I must create a profile, adjust my microphone and perform an audio check before I can begin using speech recognition.**

1. Say **SCRATCH THAT** to erase the words you said after your last pause.

2. Say **UNDO THAT** to cancel the SCRATCH THAT command and bring the erased words back.

3. Dictate the last sentence again without stopping between any words. (Notice when you say **SCRATCH THAT,** the entire line is erased).

4. Dictate the first sentence again, but this time pause between each word. (Notice when you say **SCRATCH THAT,** only one word or section will be erased).

5. Say **SELECT PARAGRAPH, DELETE THAT**

6. Dictate the paragraph again and practice with the • **UNDO THAT** and • **CANCEL THAT** commands. Notice how these commands respond differently.

7. Say **SELECT PARAGRAPH,** • **DELETE THAT**

8. Dictate the paragraph again. Without pausing between words, say "**RESUME WITH microphone.**" Notice this erases your text back to the word microphone. Experiment with these quick correction commands as you dictate in the next exercises.

5.7 More Practice Dictating and Correcting

CORRECT Command VS **SELECT Command**. You will notice these two commands are very similar.

Dictate the following sentence **pausing** as indicated after each phrase.

The two employees (*pause*) **went to the** (*pause*) **office to** (*pause*) **many times.**

Say "**CORRECT**" <to> Notice, just like when you say the "Select Command" each occurrence of the word "to" is numbered. You would still say Choose <#> to pick the correct choice.

Th❶two·employees·wer❷to·the·offic❸to·many·times.¶

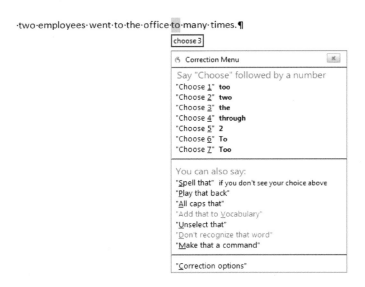

Say Choose 1 to replace ❸to·many to **too** many.

• NEW LINE VS **• NEW PARAGRAPH**

The **• NEW LINE** command moves the cursor to the next line without leaving a blank line. **• NEW PARAGRAPH** leaves a blank line between lines. **Tip***: If NEW LINE does not seem to work for you, try saying "PRESS ENTER"*

(Notice, when you say **• NEW PARAGRAPH**, the first word of the next line will automatically be capitalized. If you say**• NEW LINE,** the next line will not be capitalized UNLESS you have an ending punctuation mark at the end of the line such as a period. Without a punctuation mark, the software interprets the next line to be a continuation of the same sentence)

Start a new document. Say **NEW DOCUMENT** to open a blank Word page

1. Dictate the following sentences saying **NEW LINE** vs. **NEW PARAGRAPH** at the end of each sentence. (Be sure to dictate the ending punctuation marks.)

   The two employees went to the office too many times.

   Once upon a time, in a land far, far away, there lived a green giant.

   Once again, in the heat of the night, the fish were biting.

   As the saying goes, by the light of the moon, it happened one night.

   Over and over again, between the lines, it was often said.

   When in doubt, discuss the options and plan accordingly.

   The two employees went to the office too many times.

   He wants to go to the Olympics once in his life.

   Mr. Wright will write the right instructions on the assignment.

   They're on their way there.

   To improve your accuracy, always correct every mistake you make.

   Don't leave errors up in the air!

   I have already checked and they are all ready.

   Can I advise you on the advice you are giving to others?

   I don't know whether you have noticed, but the weather is awful today!

   He threw the ball through the target.

2. Proofread and make all corrections using the "Correct" command VS "Select" command. Try correcting phrases instead of just individual words.

3. Now try this more complex paragraph. Be sure to say the hyphen between the words *voice* and *writers* in the following way: *voice hyphen writers.*

   NEW PARAGRAPH

   Eventually, writers learned to type and entered their thoughts into typing machines at a trot, or even a gallop, to the rhythmic tapping of their fingers across the keyboard. By comparison, voice-writers produce copy at a run. Learning to think, compose, speak clearly, and edit at the speed of speech takes effort and rehearsal.

4. Proofread this paragraph and make all corrections using the "Correct" or "Select" command. *If you are unable to correct the error using the correct or select command steps fix the mistakes with the keyboard for now. You will learn to correct these more difficult errors later.*

5. Save your document: Say "**SAVE DOCUMENT AS.**" With the cursor in the filename box, say "**chapter 5 point 7 exercise.**" Say "**CLICK SAVE**"

5.8 Using Spell That to Make Corrections

What if you use the • **SELECT** or • **CORRECT** command and the correct word is not on the Quick Correction list? Restating a word may work. If you have misspoken the word or stumbled over its pronunciation, it is likely that the correct word will appear when you just say it. However, if it is still incorrect, you can use the • **SPELL THAT** command.

The **SPELL THAT** command allows you to enter the correct word or phrase by spelling it with your voice or typing it in the spelling window. By saying "**TRAIN**", Dragon is able to identify your pronunciation of the correct word and compare it to what it had originally transcribed.

Note: If you enter a word in the Spelling window that is unknown to Dragon, Dragon adds the word to its Vocabulary.

Sample:

pains of repetitive stress energy came early in life¶

In this sample the word **energy** should be **injury**. Notice injury did not show up as a choice on the choose list.

Saying **Spell That** brings up the Spelling window. The correct word "injury" was typed in the box.

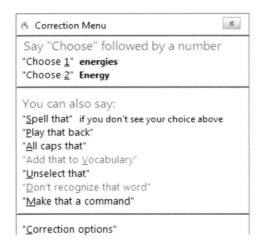

Say or Click **Train**, Say or Click **Go**, Pronounce the Word, Say or Click **Done**

Using the SPELL THAT command and following these steps any time a word or phrase does not appear in the correction list will help Dragon recognize more words and greatly improve your accuracy.

5.9 Spelling Practice

Dragon NaturallySpeaking will let you spell words instead of typing with a keyboard. This can be done:

- In the Spell That window
- When adding new words to your dictionary
- By switching to Spell Mode

In this training you will learn how to spell and recognize words letter by letter directly into your document. In other exercises, you will add and train new words that are not in the Dragon dictionary in the *Add Word* dialog box. There will also be times when you can switch into Dragon's SPELL MODE to enter in a particularly difficult word.

Spelling Tips

- Spell briskly. Don't hesitate between letters. Spell with confidence.
- Dragon actually understands you better if you spell naturally and continuously, rather than one letter at a time.
- Use the military or phonetic alphabet when certain letters do not cooperate.
- Use the • **SPACE** command to put a space between two words.
- Use • **BACKSPACE** to delete a letter to the left. Say • **BACKSPACE 2,** or • **BACKSPACE 5** or • **BACKSPACE 20** to delete multiple characters to the left.

Say "**SPELL THAT**" to bring up the Spelling Window

1. Spell George Washington by saying each letter. Begin with "Cap G"

    - **CAP** G e o r g e • **SPACE• CAP** W a s h i n g t o n
    - **PRESS ENTER**
    - **PRESS ENTER**

2.   Spell Martin Luther King by saying:

    - **CAP** M a r t i n • **SPACE** • **CAP** L u t h e r • **SPACE• CAP** K i n g
    - **PRESS ENTER**
    - **PRESS ENTER**

3. Erase by saying:
    - **BACKSPACE**
    - **BACKSPACE**
    - **BACKSPACE 4**
    - **BACKSPACE 12**
    - **CLEAR DOCUMENT**

Spelling by voice can be tricky and can take some extra practice. Many people feel that they can type the words faster than they can spell them letter by letter. It is okay to use your keyboard or mouse any time it is faster. You will get more opportunities to practice spelling.

5.10 Vocabulary Editor

One of the most important features in Dragon NaturallySpeaking is the Vocabulary Editor. Open the Vocabulary Editor by Saying •**Open Vocabulary Editor or** choosing **Vocabulary menu, Open Vocabulary Editor**

This is a list of all the words in the Dragon Speech dictionary. You can select any word and click **TRAIN** to reinforce how you pronounce the word or symbol.

This is also the place to add unique words or symbols that you want formatted in a special way. Just type the word in the written form exactly as you want it to appear and click **Add** and then **Train**. (The spoken field is used only if you want to pronounce the word or phrase differently than you write it).

By choosing **Custom words only** from the DISPLAY drop-down menu, you will limit the number of choices by listing only the words you have added to the dictionary.

If any partial words or misspelled words were accidentally added to the vocabulary, select them and press delete to remove them in the Vocabulary Editor. You can also retrain any words that are not recognized.

Don't expect perfection. The beginning goal is to get use to dictating instead of typing. Remember, don't try to correct as you dictate. Go back and proofread and make corrections just like you would if you typed the information. Taking the time to **Add** and **Train** misrecognized words and phrases can greatly increase your overall accuracy.

5.11 Practice Exercise: Dictating and Editing

Say "Start Microsoft Word"

Do not dictate the words in italics. Say [Press Enter or New Line] at the end of the sentence. Correct all misrecognized words.

Dictate the following sentences and paragraphs.

Using speech recognition software can save me time.
I must adjust my microphone so it will work correctly.
If I speak clearly, the computer will not make very many mistakes. [New Paragraph]

Dictate and edit the following sentences by voice according to instructions.

Betsy Ross is known for making American flags.
(*Change Betsy Ross to Betty Crocker*) (*insert the phrase* , a fictional character, *after Betty Crocker—don't forget the commas*)
(*Change American flags to apple pies*)
[Move right 1] (or Move right one character)
[New Line]

I just got back from a trip to San Antonio, Texas. While I was there, I visited the Alamo.
(*Change San Antonio, Texas to Orlando, Florida*)
(*Change* the Alamo *to* my friends at Disney World, Mickey Mouse and Goofy*)*.
[Move right 1] (or Move right one character)
[New Paragraph]

Dictate the following Preamble of the United States Constitution making all corrections by voice (don't forget the commas):
We the people of the United States, in order to form a more perfect union, establish justice, insure domestic tranquility, provide for the common defense, promote the general welfare, and secure the blessings of liberty to ourselves and our posterity, do ordain and establish this Constitution for the United States of America.

Practice moving around the document by speaking the following commands:
[Go to top]
[Select line][Delete that]
[Insert after known for making] delicious
[Move right two words]
[Select apple pies] [Unselect that]
[Go to bottom]
[Move up 3 lines][Move right 4 characters] [Move left 2 words] [Move up 2 lines] [Beginning of line][Go to top] [Go to bottom] [Insert before common defense]
Save as: *dictating and editing*
[Clear document]

CHAPTER 6—REINFORCING DICTATION SKILLS

Numbers are also easy to dictate. In most cases you can dictate them as you would normally say them. Dates, phone numbers, currency, zip codes and times of day will often appear in the correct format. If you have trouble when dictating single numbers, say the word **"press"** or "**numeral**" before dictating the number.

Note: The "Format That Number" "Format That Spelled Out" and "Abbreviated" commands are no longer supported in Dragon Version 12. Number formatting and abbreviations are now set in the **Auto-Formatting** dialog box.

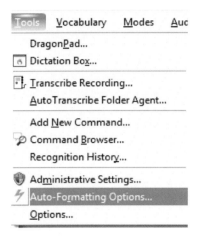

Notice the items that are checked by default.

In this example: many items are marked to automatically format.

Dragon will type the actual numbers that are greater or equal to 10 and words for numbers below 10.

When dictating numbers:

To enter	Say
4	"four" or "numeral four"
23	"twenty three"
179	"one hundred seventy nine," "one hundred and seventy nine," *or* "one seventy nine"
5,423	"five comma thousand four twenty three"
142,015	"one hundred forty two thousand and fifteen"
127,400,042	"one hundred twenty seven million four-hundred thousand forty-two"
$45	"forty five dollars"
$99.50	"ninety nine dollars and fifty cents"
8:30 p.m.	"eight thirty pm"
May 15, 2003	"May fifteen comma two thousand three" (note: saying "comma" is optional)
Oakland, CA 99077	"Oakland California 99077"

6.1   Dictating Numbers

Practice dictating numbers. You can dictate the following across the screen by saying "**tab key**" after each entry or you can list them underneath each other by saying "**enter**". *Remember, you can use the **Select** or **Correct** command and **choose** corrections from the correction list for numbers also.

Numbers:

12   35   60   125   750   3143   5,185,000   3 (numeral 3)

Currency:

Dictate the following currency by saying (_____dollars and _____ cents) Example: (Seven dollars and 75 cents *will show* $7.75)

$5.15 [Tab key] $123.25 $1366 $1,350,000

Dates:

Dictate the following dates. Just say month, day, year together and you will not need to say the comma. To dictate the numeric form say "slash" for the /.

February 14, 1996   2/14/1996
May 16, 2001   5/16/2001
August 21, 2010   8/24/2010

Times:

Dictate the following times by saying the time along with AM or PM: (Don't worry if the format is not identical).

1:30 PM   5:15 PM   10:10 PM   6:20AM   3:45 AM

Phone Numbers:

Dictate the following phone numbers without saying the hyphens: (Don't hesitate between the numbers)

472-4564   602-334-5678
555-1212   309-682-0544
480-472-0395   1-800-749-1844

ZIP Codes:

Dictate the following zip codes. Say the city, full state name, and zip together--you do not need to say "comma". Dragon will change the state to a two letter abbreviation.

61615   89121   Mesa, AZ 85205   Boston, MA 02460

Save your document: Say "**Save Document AS**", with the cursor in the File Name box, Say "**chapter 6 point 1 exercise**", Say "**Click Save**".

6.2 Dictating Punctuation and Symbols

Turn on your microphone. Practice saying the following special characters.

hyplen —

	• APOSTROPHE		• COPYRIGHT SIGN	
	• APOSTROPHE S		• TRADEMARK SIGN	
	• BACK SLASH		• REGISTERED SIGN	
	• OPEN BRACKET		• NUMBER SIGN	
	• CLOSE BRACKET		• PERCENT SIGN	
	• OPEN QUOTE		• OPEN ANGLE BRACKET	
	• CLOSE QUOTE		• LESS THAN SIGN	
	• DASH		• CLOSE ANGLE BRACKET	
	• ELLIPSIS · · ·		• GREATER THAN SIGN	
	• OPEN PAREN		• AMPERSAND	
	• CLOSE PAREN	—	• UNDERSCORE	
	• TILDE (til-dah) ~		• VERTICAL BAR	
	• AT SIGN @		• PLUS SIGN	
	• EURO SIGN		• EQUALS SIGN	
	• EXCLAIMATION MARK		• QUESTION MARK	

m dash

— *minus sign*

Puzzled? If you have trouble with any symbol or punctuation, you can train it. Say • **OPEN VOCABULARY EDITOR,** or choose **Open Vocabulary Editor from the Dragon Bar, Vocabulary** menu. Type the symbol in the **Written form:** box. Notice that the symbol with the correct pronunciation will appear. Click **Train** and train the word. (*See Section 6.4 for more information on the Vocabulary Editor*)

Try This:
Although there are many spoken choices for they symbol " -- *quotation mark* is not listed. You can add the spoken form *quotation mark* to the list by typing it in the spoken form box and then click **Add**, then **Train**.

Say **Open Vocabulary Editor**   Type **"**in Written form and Quotation Mark in Spoken form.

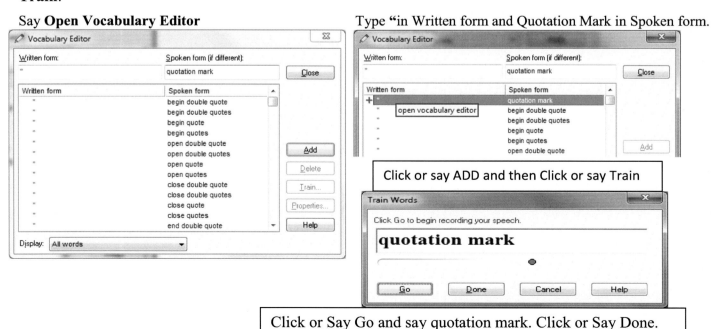

Open chapter 6.1 exercise if it is not already open. Add the following sentences or phrases to this exercise. (You may need to refer to the special characters chart on the previous page and review dictation tips for dictating numbers.) Remember to dictate the entire sentences, do not try to correct as you dictate. Numbers and symbols can be awkward to dictate at first, so be patient.

Tammy paid $4.25 for paper, pencils, and pens.

My birthday is November 10.

"I am freezing," she said. "It is only 37° in here!"

Today's date is (*say today's month date and year*).

I earned $25.50 for babysitting last night.

School starts at 8:05 AM and ends at 2:55 PM each day.

They have 35 horses, 20 fish, 5 cats, 7 birds and 2 hamsters.

Her address is 525 E. Brown, Atlanta, GA 78235.

His phone number is 888-352-1761.

Coca-Cola™

*Required fields

30*5 = 150

360/12 = 30

©2009   **(Hint:** *say copyright sign no space* **2009)**

$32,865.25

35%

[Johnson & Johnson...]

500 >300 (*be sure to say greater than sign or it may write out greater than*)

725 < 837

250+25 -100 = 175

Proofread and **correct** all the above sentences and phrases using the **Select** Command. **Save** your document:

Say "**Save Document AS**", with the cursor in the filename box, Say "**chapter 6 point 2 exercise**", Say "**Click Save**"

Print the file by saying **PRINT THE FILE**. Notice the print dialog box will appear. Check settings and say **OK**.

6.3 Capitalization & Compounding Words

The classic Dragon NaturallySpeaking capitalization commands are:
CAP THAT or CAPITALIZE THAT-- for initial capital letters
NO CAPS THAT – for lowercase letters
ALL CAPS THAT – for all uppercase letters

If you need to put two words together, use • **COMPOUND THAT.** For example, if you want the word *"everybody"* and *"every body"* appears, you can select the words and say • **COMPOUND THAT.** Some corporations put two or more words together to form their logo such as Dragon NaturallySpeaking.

Complete the following exercise to practice capitalization and compounding commands.

Say   **Training words and phrases**

Say • **CAP THAT**   ✓

Say • **NO CAPS THAT**

Say • **ALL CAPS THAT**

Say • **LOWERCASE THAT**

Say • **CAPITALIZE THAT**

Say • **NEW LINE   Using natural capitalization**

Say • **SELECT Using natural capitalization**

Say • **UPPERCASE THAT**

Say • **SELECT SENTENCE**

Say • **LOWERCASE THAT**

Say • **SELECT LINE**

Say • **UNSELECT THAT**

Complete the following exercise using the COMPOUND THAT command

Say • **speaking solutions**

Say • **CAP THAT**

Say •**COMPOUND THAT.**

Say • **Soft Scan**

Say • **COMPOUND THAT**

Say • **UPPERCASE THAT**

Say • **Clear Document** *to erase screen*

6.4   Add and Train Words

In the last chapter, you learned to use the **Spell That** command to add unique words to the user dictionary. This is a quick way to add words when you are proofreading and correcting misrecognized words within a document. Another way to add unique words, names and phrases to your own user dictionary is to use the ADD WORD command or OPEN VOCABULARY EDITOR. If you have troublesome words or unique names that you are going to use over and over again, it is best to add and train them using the following steps:

A. Say • **ADD WORD,** or choose **Vocabulary** menu, **Add New Word or Phrase**.

B. Type or spell the word, phrase, or name letter-by-letter.

C. Say or click • **ADD** to train the name, word, or phrase. (*If a word sounds different than it is spelled you can key how it sounds under spoken form otherwise leave it blank*)

D. Say or click • **GO.** Wait briefly for the microphone to activate, then say the word, phrase, or name the exact way you intend to say it in the future. Say • **DONE** to continue.

   Follow the steps in A-D to add the following words:

Kasey Bloomindale (*notice no "g"***)**
Wowzer
bibbidybobbidyboo
oinkers
Your first and last name
Name of your school or company (*be sure to include proper capitalization***)**

After you add these words, say the words in Microsoft Word to see if they come out correctly. If any of them are not correct, select the word and use SPELL THAT, TRAIN.

Say **Open Vocabulary Editor**—start spelling or typing supercalif… notice words are listed alphabetically and supercalifragilisticexpialidocious is already in the Dragon dictionary. However, this is a mouthful to say. You can abbreviate how you want to say a word by keying it in the spoken form box.

Type super cal in the <u>spoken</u> form: Click Add

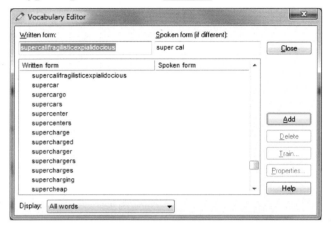 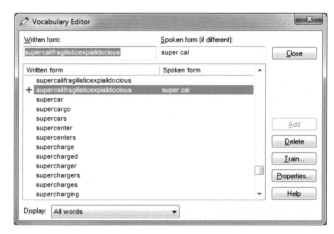

Click Train—Click GO…say super cal, Click Done

Now, say **super cal** and the computer should type: **supercalifragilisticexpialidocious.** (*You are telling the computer to type out the written form when you say the spoken form*)**.** Try 2 more:

<u>Written Form</u>	<u>Spoken Form</u>
Skyline High School	**SHS**
<u>email@yahoo.com</u> **(use your e-mail)**	**work e-mail**

Start a new document and dictate the following sentences using the words you just added.

My name is (*your name*).
My best friend is (*friend's first and last name*).
Kasey Bloomindale has a dog named Wowzer.
The pigs were called oinkers in the story.
Cinderella's fairy godmother chanted bibbidybobbidyboo.
I go to school (*or work*) **at** (*name of your school or company name*).
My sister goes to SHS (computer will spell out Skyline High School).
My e-mail address is work e-mail (computer will write your e-mail address).
Proofread, make all corrections and **Save Document As** "**chapter 6 point 5 exercise**".

6.5　Starter Sentences

A great way to improve your voice-writing skills is to dictate complete sentences. In this next exercise you will see a list of starter sentences and you must complete the thought or idea. Think about what you want to say before you turn on your microphone. Use the "CORRECT" command to choose any corrections and use the SPELL THAT command to correct any words that do not appear on the Correction List. (Say NEW PARAGRAPH after each sentence).

My name is...

Today is ...

My phone number is...(do not pause or say hyphens when dictating your phone number)

My birthday is . . .

I attend school at ...

My home address is ...

My favorite food is...

I am most happy when...

The most important thing to me is...

I am very lucky to have...

(Keep this document open and follow the steps below for Activity 6.6.)

6.6　Compare Speech to Typing

1. Start a **NEW PARAGRAPH** and warm up by dictating this dialogue. Correct any mistakes.

   Using speech recognition is fun. Dragon NaturallySpeaking is easy to learn. Start by speaking in simple sentences. Remember to say punctuation. Dragon wants you to speak naturally. Do not stop between words or break words into syllables. Speak to your computer the way television news personalities read the news.

2. Dictate this dialog again as clearly as you can. Time yourself to see how long it takes or have someone time you as you speak. Don't rush! Speak clearly and evenly.

   Using speech recognition is fun. Dragon NaturallySpeaking is easy to learn. Start by speaking in simple sentences. Remember to say punctuation. Dragon wants you to speak naturally. Do not stop between words or break words into syllables. Speak to your computer the way television news personalities read the news. • NEW PARAGRAPH • MICROPHONE OFF

3. Take a minute and warm up your keyboarding skills, then time yourself using the keyboard to type the same dialogue seen above. Do not correct any mistakes as you type, then compare speed and accuracy.

4. Save your document: Say "**SAVE DOCUMENT AS**", with the cursor in the File Name box, Say "**chapter 6 point 6 exercise**", Say "**Click SAVE**

6.7   Timed Writing-- Evaluating Speed and Accuracy

In traditional keyboarding classes, teachers normally count every five characters as a word. This formula makes evaluating typing ability consistent from typist to typist. The formula counts spaces. Chances are, based on the keyboarding formula; you are already speaking 110-140 words per minute or even faster!

Take a one minute timing on the following paragraphs by voice. Keep your eyes on the text and do not look at the screen as you read. Do not stop at the end of a line but just keep reading through the entire paragraph. Do NOT stop or correct any errors. When the minute is up turn off your microphone, proofread and indicate your wpm/errors.

	wpm
(*Tab key*) **Credit cards can make shopping very convenient, and they**	12
can help you keep track of the money you spend. Some items	24
such as renting a car or staying in a hotel may require a	36
customer to use a credit card. However, many card companies	48
and banks charge high fees for using their credit cards. (*NEW LINE*)	60
(*Tab key*)**You must realize that it may be better to pay in cash**	70
and not use a credit card. If you apply for a credit card,	82
you should shop for the best credit terms. Some card	93
companies do not charge yearly fees. Some may offer you	104
benefits such as extended warranties or money back on the	116
merchandise you buy with their credit cards. Read the fine	128
print and evaluate all the information. You may be surprised	140
at the differences between the terms of various credit cards. (*NEW LINE*)	152
(*Tab key*)**Some credit cards are now being marketed to children.**	163
Parents now can obtain a credit card that is intended for	175
children as young as six years old. There is a transaction	187
fee every time the card is used. In addition, there is a	199
yearly fee and an additional fee each time the card is used.	211

1 |2 |3 |4 |5 |6 |7 |8 |9 |10 |11 |12

Now, take a one minute timing on the same paragraphs by using the keyboard. Keep your eyes on the text and do not look at the screen as you type. Do NOT backspace or correct any errors. When the minute is up turn off your microphone, proofread and indicate your wpm/errors.

Save your document: Say "**SAVE DOCUMENT AS**", with the cursor in the File Name box, Say "**chapter 6 point 7 exercise**", Say "**Click Save**". Say **Print the File** and notice the print dialog box will appear. Check settings and say **OK**.

Additional timed writings can be taken from any other keyboarding resource.

6.8 Read That and Play That Back

Dragon NaturallySpeaking includes a text-to-speech feature that allows your text to be read in a synthesized voice or played back in your own voice. This is very beneficial for editing or reviewing documents. You can have the contents of a document read to you or listen for mistakes in your writing. Be sure your speakers or headset is properly configured to hear text-to-speech. You can choose **Play that Back** or **Read That** from the **Audio menu** or use one of the following commands.

- **READ THAT**
- **READ PARAGRAPH**
- **READ FROM HERE**
- **READ TO HERE**
- **PLAY BACK**
- **PLAY BACK TO HERE**
- **PLAY BACK FROM HERE**

➢ You can control the speed, pitch, volume, and other aspects of text-to-speech output. Set these options in the <u>Options Playback/Text-to-speech tab</u>.

➢ You can simultaneously stop playback and open the Correction menu by pressing the minus key (-) on the numeric keypad. The last phrase played appears in the dialog box for you to correct.

➢ To stop the reading or play back, press the Escape Key.

Dictate this paragraph:

Training is essential for successful use of speech recognition software. An individual must learn to adjust the microphone properly, create a speech profile, and learn how to speak clearly to the computer to optimize recognition. The user must also learn the operational procedures of the software. Most individuals are surprised at how fast and how accurately they can type my voice after only a few hours of practice.

1. Say •**SELECT PARAGRAPH**

2. Say • **READ THAT** (or use the mouse to choose **Read That** from the **Audio** menu) to have the entire paragraph read in a synthesized voice.

3. When it is about halfway through the paragraph, press the **Escape Key** to stop the reading.

4. Say • **INSERT BEFORE Most** (*notice cursor moves to the beginning of last sentence*)

5. Say • **PLAY BACK FROM HERE**.

6. Select different sections of this paragraph and experiment with the READ THAT or PLAY THAT BACK commands. (These will be useful commands when proofreading in the future).

CHAPTER 7—USING COMMANDS

You should now have a good understanding of the dictation basics of using Dragon NaturallySpeaking. The next chapters will focus on using more commands for navigating and formatting documents.

Using speech recognition software doesn't mean that everything needs to be hands-free. Many people prefer to navigate and edit their documents with their keyboard or mouse. However, as you become more familiar with Dragon features, you may find it beneficial to use more voice commands.

The Sidebar displays automatically when you open a Dragon User Profile by default. However, you were asked to close the Dragon Sidebar when working through previous chapters because it was important for you to learn the dictation basics first.

Don't try to memorize a lot of commands. You will learn what commands are more useful for you as you dictate and become more familiar with using Dragon NaturallySpeaking with a variety of programs. The voice commands will become a natural part of your dictation the more you use them.

7.1 Dragon Sidebar

The Dragon Sidebar shows a list of sample commands that can be used for whatever program you are using. A list of global commands appears if there is no list of specific commands available for a particular program. Many people find this SideBar very helpful, and others find it distracting. Just like using the task pane in other programs, it is a personal preference whether to have the Sidebar showing or not.

If the **Sidebar** is closed, you can open it from the DragonBar **Help Menu** OR Say "SHOW DRAGON SIDEBAR"

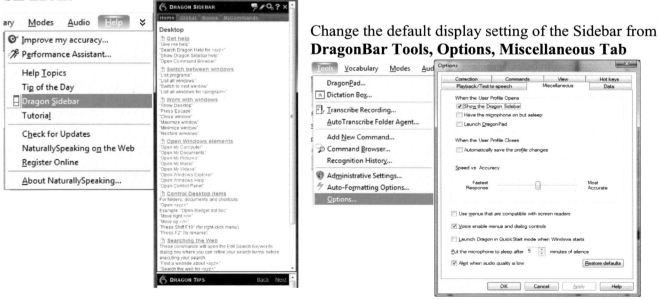

Change the default display setting of the Sidebar from **DragonBar Tools, Options, Miscellaneous Tab**

7.2   Docking the Dragon Sidebar

By right clicking on the DragonBar, you can dock the Sidebar on the left or right side of the screen, set it to auto-hide, or set it to "float" like other windows, and place it anywhere you want on the Windows Desktop. if the Sidebar covers up part of your document, you may want to change the Zoom percentage to 90%.

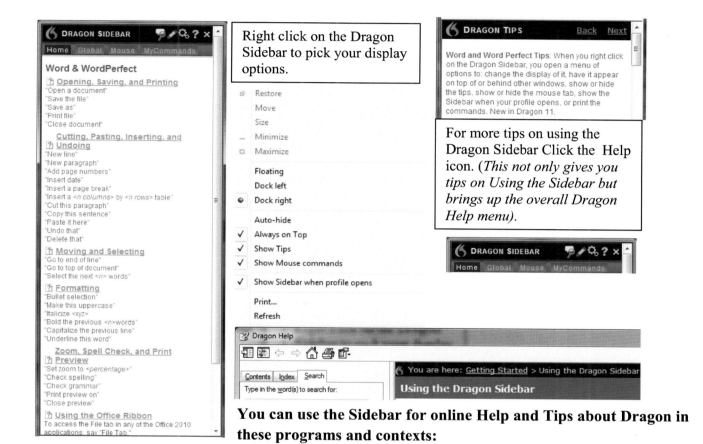

You can use the Sidebar for online Help and Tips about Dragon in these programs and contexts:

- Desktop commands
- Global commands
- DragonBar, DragonPad, Dictation Box, Spelling Window, Command Browser
- Microsoft Word, Microsoft Excel, Microsoft Outlook, Microsoft Outlook Express, Windows Mail, Microsoft PowerPoint, and Microsoft InfoPath
- Corel WordPerfect
- Lotus Notes
- OpenOffice.org Writer
- Internet Explorer and Mozilla Firefox

7.3   Viewing the Dragon Sidebar and Switching Between Programs

When switching between programs, you will notice the Dragon Sidebar will automatically show commands for the active screen.

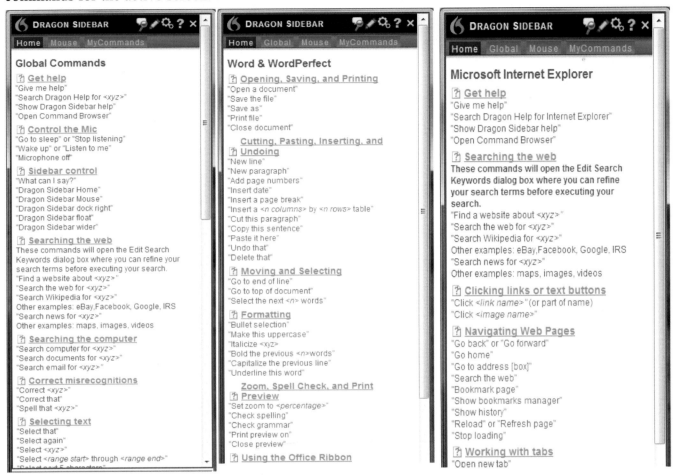

1.   Say "**SHOW DRAGON SIDEBAR**" if Sidebar is not showing.

2.   Say • **START MICROSOFT WORD** to open Word. Notice the Sample Commands window now reflects commands in Word & Word Perfect.

3.   Say • **START INTERNET EXPLORER** to view the Dragon Sidebar commands in Internet Explorer.

4.   Say • **SWITCH TO WORD** notice this will toggle back to the Word window and Word sample commands will appear in the Sidebar

5.   Say • **SWITCH TO INTERNET EXPLORER** to switch back to the internet window.

6.   Say • **START MICROSOFT EXCEL** to open Excel. Notice the Sample Commands window now reflects commands in Excel.

7.   Practice switching back and forth between open windows and look at how the Dragon Sidebar commands change.

8.   Say • **CLOSE WINDOW** to close and exit each program by voice

7.4 Dragon Classic Commands VS. Natural Language Commands

Dragon Classic Commands are standard Dragon commands that work with all applications and are usually dictated immediately after saying a phrase or by using the "SELECT" command. Dragon Natural Language Commands, allow you to avoid the multiple menu-selection and mouse-movement steps associated with the traditional Classic Dragon Commands interface. Instead of requiring users to memorize a specific command such as "BOLD THAT," the new Natural Language Commands recognize a wide variety of ways in which a user may issue a command "MAKE THAT BOLD," "BOLD THE LAST PARAGRAPH," "SET FONT BOLD" all will accomplish the same task.

Because the number of valid commands is so large, you should just try saying what you want to do. If you get unexpected results, say "Undo That" to undo the action and try another way to say the command. You can also look at the suggested commands in the Dragon Sidebar.

Steps for checking the Natural Command Settings—Tools, Options, Commands Tab

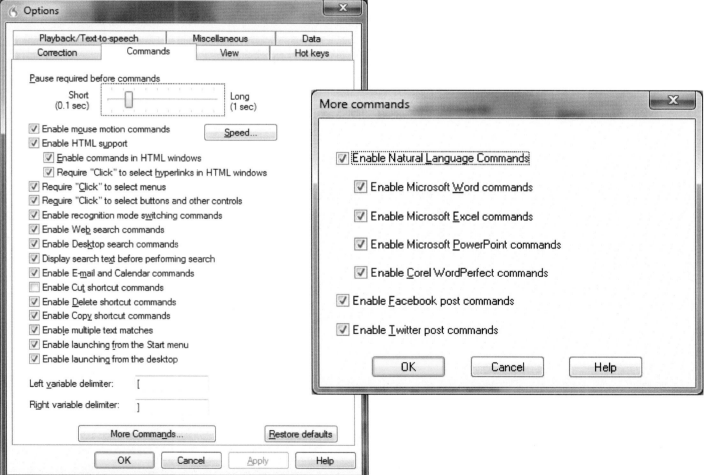

7.5 Practicing Formatting Commands

1. Use Classic and Natural Commands to Bold, Italicize, & Underline Text

    To bold, italicize, or underline text after it has already been dictated, you can either select the text and say the Classic Command such as • SELECT *<word/phrase>*, •BOLD THAT, or you can use a Natural Command such as •BOLD *<word/phrase>*, or •ITALICIZE *<word/phrase>*.

    Dictate the paragraph below without formatting. Follow instructions below the paragraph to practice Classic and Natural commands.

    Learning to <u>format</u> with your *voice* is easy. You just need to know the <u>proper commands</u> for what you want the *computer* to do. It is actually best to <u>format</u> your document after you dictate your text instead of trying to <u>format</u> as you are dictating.

    - Say •SELECT voice, Say •BOLD THAT, • ITALICIZE THAT
    - Say •SELECT proper commands, •UNDERLINE THAT
    - Say •BOLD Learning, Say •ITALICIZE computer
    - Say •UNDERLINE format (*notice all three occurrences of the word format will appear*) say •CHOOSE ALL and all of them will be underlined. If you only wanted one underlined, you would just choose that number.

2. Use the • RESTORE THAT command to return bold, italicized, or underlined text to normal. Practice the • RESTORE THAT command on the same paragraph.

    - Say •SELECT Learning, •RESTORE THAT (bold is removed)
    - Say SELECT voice •RESTORE THAT, (bold and italics are removed)
    - Say •SELECT PARAGRAPH, •RESTORE THAT (all formatting is removed)
    - Say •UNDO THAT (previous formatting will reappear).

3. Use •SELECT <word/phrase> THROUGH <word/phrase> commands to select long passages of text without saying each and every word. Use the • UNSELECT THAT command to deselect selected text

    - Say •SELECT It is THROUGH dictating, Say •ALL CAP THAT

      for what you want the *computer* to do. IT IS ACTUALLY BEST TO FORMAT YOUR DOCUMENT AFTER YOU DICTATE YOUR TEXT INSTEAD OF TRYING TO FORMAT AS YOU ARE DICTATING. ¶

    - Say •SELECT know THROUGH do, Say •UNSELECT THAT
    - Say •SELECT first sentence, Say •BOLD THAT

      Learning to format with your voice is easy. You just need to know the <u>proper commands</u> for what you want the *computer* to do. It is actually best to <u>format</u> your document after

4. Use •BULLET THAT, •FORMAT THAT BULLET STYLE and •NUMBER THAT commands to create bulleted and numbered lists.

You can dictate the first item and then say the •**BULLET THAT** or •**NUMBER THAT** command OR you can select all items after dictating and then apply the •**BULLET THAT** or •**NUMBER THAT** command. It is a personal preference.

Say •**CLEAR DOCUMENT** and dictate the following list:

Speech recognition: • **NEW LINE**
increases productivity • **NEW LINE**
improves communication skills • **NEW LINE**
helps prevent repetitive stress injuries • **NEW LINE**

Say •**SELECT previous 3 lines**, Say • **BULLET THAT** to create bullets
Say • **NUMBER THAT** to change from bullets to numbers

Say **CLEAR DOCUMENT** and dictate the following list:

My favorite foods are: • **NEW LINE**
pizza •**BULLET THAT,** • **NEW LINE**
chocolate ice cream • **NEW LINE**
peanut butter and jelly sandwiches • **NEW LINE**

Say •**BULLETS OFF** to turn off bullets and return cursor to left margin. (Or, say **PRESS ENTER, PRESS ENTER** to turn off bullets to start a new paragraph at left margin**.**)

5. Use •**CENTER THAT, •LEFT ALIGN THAT, or •RIGHT ALIGN THAT** to align text to the left margin, center of the document or to the right margin.

Say right-hand man, Say •**RIGHT ALIGN THAT**, then Say •**NEW LINE**
central station, Say •**CAP THAT, •CENTER THAT, •NEW LINE**)
Lefty Jones •**LEFT ALIGN THAT, •NEW LINE**)

The results should look like this in your document:

right-hand man

Central Station

Lefty Jones

Notice when you dictated the alignment commands, the next line stayed at the alignment you dictated until you said a new alignment command. You can also apply alignment commands to individual text passages by first selecting the text.

Try this to see how the selected text will change alignment with each command:

Say •**SELECT right-hand man, •LEFT ALIGN THAT, •CENTER THAT**

7.6 Editing and Correcting

There is a difference between *correcting misrecognitions* and *voice-editing*. When ***voice-editing,*** you will fix *your* mistakes. At times, every writer will stumble over their words, change their mind, or use the wrong words for the tone of a particular paragraph. These errors cannot be blamed on the software. Nevertheless, they need to be edited. Learning to edit with your voice can be a huge timesaver and can improve your writing.

Fortunately, when using speech recognition software, spelling errors will be minimal, even absent from your writing. Dragon may misrecognize what you are saying and type the wrong word, but it *will* be spelled correctly! As far as the use of homonyms, the speech software makes logical guesses based on the context of the words in the sentence.

However, for this context checking feature to work properly, you must practice speaking in complete sentences and phrases. Speaking in full, uninterrupted sentences and phrases helps the software guess which part of speech, which homonym, or which spelling of the word you need typed. Sometimes it makes a difference in where you pause when speaking.

Example Phrase: As you work for higher speed in keyboarding

If you pause after the word **higher** before saying **speed**, you may get the word **hire** instead of **higher** because hire is grammatically correct. If you say **higher speed** together without pausing between the words, the computer will not make this mistake. (Experiment with this sentence yourself).

7.7 Practice Editing

Dictate the following paragraph and then follow the steps below to practice editing.

People have the ability to carry on conversations and tell stories. Almost everyone can relate a story and say something meaningful. And now they have the software to turn their speech into words.

1. Say • **INSERT BEFORE** *ability to carry.* Pause briefly and say: **special**
2. Say • **UNDERLINE** conversations
3. Say • **Delete** Almost
4. Say • **Capitalize Everyone**
5.   Say • **INSERT AFTER** relate a story, Say *comma* **express a point of view** *comma*
6. Say • **SELECT** *speech into words.* Pause briefly and say:
    most important thoughts into a written form
7. Compare your paragraph to the one below.

1   2   3-4
People have the **special** ability to carry on <u>conversations</u> and tell stories. Everyone can
5
relate a story, **express a point of view,** and say something meaningful. And now they have
                                       6
the software to turn their **most important thoughts into a written form.**

CHAPTER 8—APPLYING DICTATION, CORRECTION & FORMATTING COMMANDS

In the previous chapters, you learned many of the speech recognition dictation basics, correction strategies and formatting commands. You will practice applying these concepts when creating the following documents. **Remember it takes time and practice!**

- Tune your microphone **"CHECK AUDIO"**
- Dictate the text of the document first and then edit and format the text.
- Don't watch the screen when you dictate.
- Turn off the Microphone when you are not dictating.
- Use the **"PLAY THAT BACK"** or **"READ THAT"** commands to help you proofread.
- Use the **SELECT** and **CHOOSE** command to make corrections when the correct word appears on the choose list.
- Use **SELECT and SAY** to make a correction by just repeating the word when it does not appear on the choose list.
- Use **SPELL THAT** when the correct word did not appear after trying **SELECT and SAY**. Remember you can type in the correct word instead of spelling it with your voice.
- Use the **ADD WORD** command to add a word to the vocabulary
- Use the **TRAIN WORD** to reinforce your pronunciation of a word
- Format documents as your final step.

Below are two examples of reports you will create in Chapter 8

PREVENTING COMPUTER INJURIES

Your Name

October 3, 2008

For April, Miguel, and Maria, the pains of repetitive stress injury came early in life. (The names have been changed to protect privacy.) For this trio, symptoms began in their elementary typing classes. By the time they reached the required middle school typing class, their pains were getting worse.

A Growing Problem

Repetitive Stress Injury (also known as RSI) has become a major problem. Many professionals are now at risk for RSI. For example:

- An estimated 25% of computer users will suffer some form of RSI during their careers.
- Over 1,800,000 workers have some form of RSI.
- Approximately 600,000 employees miss some work as a result of RSI.
- Using a keyboard or mouse for more than four hours a day is considered a risk factor for RSI.
- Prevention programs could eliminate 460,000 injuries every year.

THE NATURE OF VOICE WRITING

©Speaking Solutions 2001

People have the ability to carry on conversations and tell stories. Almost everyone can relate to a story and say something meaningful. And now they have the software to turn their speech into writing.

Voice-writing requires practice and lots of it. People adjust the pace of their writing to the efficiency of their input tools. In centuries past, writers would saddle their thoughts and slow them down to a walk when crafting paragraphs with pen and ink. Eventually, writers learned to type and entered their thoughts into typing machines at a trot, or even a gallop, to the rhythmic tapping of their fingers across the keyboard. By comparison, voice-writers produce copy at a run. Learning to think, compose, speak clearly, and edit at the speed of speech takes effort and rehearsal.

8.1　Dictate and Edit Short Report "Why Train Mistakes"

You will practice dictating, correcting and formatting with your voice as you create the following short report.

1.　Turn on your microphone and open Microsoft Word if necessary.

2.　Start with a clear screen. Dictate these three paragraphs separating each one with the •
NEW PARAGRAPH command.

> **Sometimes words are misspoken. With speech software, you should train each and every mistake. Always train errors. When you fix each mistake in the proper way, Dragon NaturallySpeaking remembers. This will improve your accuracy.**
>
> **You can train words or phrases. If the proper word appears in the correction list, simply choose the proper word. If the proper word does not appear in the correction list, you must spell the word. You may need to record a word or phrase that is giving you difficulty.**
>
> **Training mistakes is the most important thing you can do to improve your recognition accuracy. If you train mistakes in the way explained in this book, you will notice the improvement in accuracy each and every day.**

3.　Correct each and every mistake in the three paragraphs above using the **SELECT and SAY**, **SELECT** and **CHOOSE** or **SPELL THAT** commands. Remember you can use the "**PLAY THAT BACK**" or "**READ THAT**" commands to help you proofread. (See 5.8 Page 37)

4.　Say "**Save Document AS**", with the cursor in the filename box, Say "**Chapter 8 Why Train Mistakes**", Say "**Click Save**"

8.2　Practice Navigating/Moving Around Document

- Make sure "**Chapter 8 Why Train Mistakes**" is still open on your screen.
- Say• **GO TO TOP** to move to the top of the document.
- Say• **GO TO BOTTOM** to move to the bottom of the document.
- Say• **MOVE UP 2 LINES**
- Say• **MOVE DOWN 3 LINES**
- Say• **MOVE TO PREVIOUS PARAGRAPH**
- Say• **MOVE TO NEXT PARAGRAPH**
- Say• **MOVE RIGHT 5 WORDS**
- Say• **GO TO TOP**

8.3   Insert and Capitalize Headings

- With the cursor at the top of the document, dictate **Why Train Mistakes? • NEW PARAGRAPH**

- Say**• INSERT BEFORE You can train** (*this will move the cursor to the beginning of the second paragraph*)

- Dictate **Correction list • NEW PARAGRAPH** (*Choose the correct number if more than one is selected*)

- Say**• INSERT BEFORE Training mistakes** (*this will move the cursor to the beginning of the third paragraph*)

- Dictate **Improving accuracy• NEW PARAGRAPH**

- Say **• SELECT Why train mistakes**

- Say **• UPPERCASE THAT or ALL CAP THAT** to create a title with all capital letters

- Say **• SELECT Correction list**

- Say **• CAP THAT or CAPITALIZE THAT** to capitalize this heading

- Say **• SELECT Improving Accuracy**

- Say **• CAP THAT or CAPITALIZE THAT** to capitalize this heading

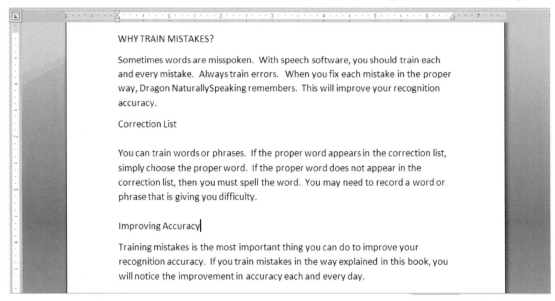

- Say **• SELECT ALL, READ THAT (Listen as the computer reads your paragraphs)**

- **Proofread, make all corrections** and **Save Document As "chapter 8 point 3 exercise".**

- Say **Print the File**, the print dialog box will appear, check printer settings and say **OK**.

8.4 Dictate, Edit and Format Report "Preventing Computer Injuries"

1. Turn on your microphone and open Microsoft Word.

2. Dictate the following paragraph. Say • **OPEN PAREN** or • **OPEN PARENTHESES** for (. Say • **CLOSE PAREN** or • **CLOSE PARENTHESES** for). Fix all the errors at the end of the paragraph.

   For April, Miguel, and Maria, the pains of repetitive stress injury came early in life. (The names have been changed to protect privacy.) For this trio, symptoms began in their elementary typing classes. By the time they reached a required middle school typing class, their pains were getting worse.

   - **NEW PARAGRAPH**

3. Say • **GO TO TOP** and add a title. Say • **NEW PARAGRAPH,** • **MOVE UP 2** to create room for the title and say:

   Preventing computer injuries

   - **ALL CAP THAT or UPPERCASE THAT**
   - **BOLD THAT**
   - **ITALICIZE THAT**
   - **UNDERLINE THAT**

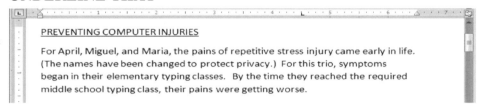

4. Say • **GO TO BOTTOM** to move to the bottom of the document. Dictate the following paragraphs. (*When dictating the numbers with decimals, say **29 point 6** for 29.6).*

   Mayo Clinic study

   - **NEW PARAGRAPH**

   As people get older, a greater percentage of the population is impacted by repetitive stress injuries. In an interesting study at the Mayo Clinic in Scottsdale, Arizona, 29.6 % of hospital respondents reported numbness, prickly sensations or abnormal sensitivity.

   - **NEW PARAGRAPH**

   Of the 257 respondents, 70 employees reported RSI related symptoms. Of those, 27 or 10.5 % were classified with carpal tunnel syndrome, which is similar to that found in the general population in past studies.

5. Bold the **Mayo Clinic Study** subtitle saying:

   - **SELECT Mayo Clinic study**
   - **BOLD THAT**
   - **CAP THAT**

6. Compare your document to the one below. Proofread and correct any mistakes using the SELECT and CHOOSE/SPELL commands. Remember, you can use the "Play that Back" or "Read that" commands to help you proofread.

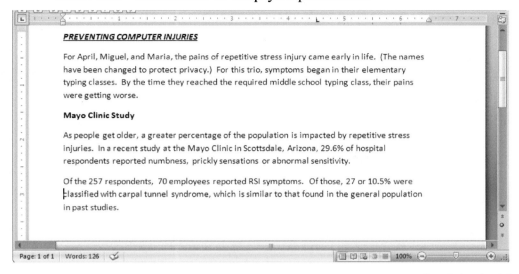

7. Say • **SELECT ALL, • RESTORE THAT** to remove all of the bolded, italicized, and underlined font styles from the document. Say • **UNSELECT THAT** to deselect the selected text.

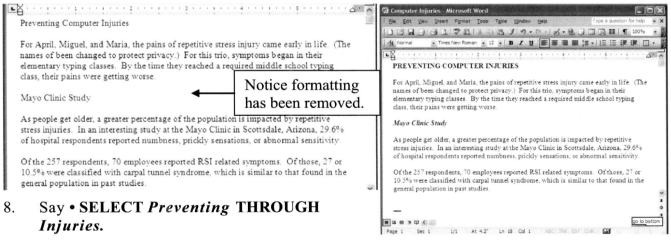

8. Say • **SELECT** *Preventing* **THROUGH** *Injuries.*

9. Say • **BOLD THAT**

10. •Say • **SELECT** *Mayo* **THROUGH** *study.*

11. Say • **BOLD THAT, • ITALICIZE THAT, • UNSELECT THAT.**

12. Say • **SAVE THE FILE** or • **FILE, • SAVE** to update your file Save your document before continuing: Say "**Save Document AS**", with the cursor in the filename box, Say "**Chapter 8 Preventing Computer Injuries**", Say **CAP THAT** to capitalize name of document "**Click Save**"

8.5 Placing Bullets

1. Be sure your **Chapter 8 Preventing Computer Injuries file** is Open.

   Say • **GO TO BOTTOM** to move to the end of the document.

2. Dictate the following. Use the • **NEW PARAGRAPH** command to separate the paragraphs/Sections with a blank line. (*Say numbers normally such as **one million eight hundred thousand** for the number **1,800,000**)*

   A Growing Problem

   Repetitive stress injury (also known as RSI) has become a major problem. Many professionals are now at risk for RSI. For example:

   An estimated 25 % of computer users will suffer some form of RSI during their careers. Over 1,800,000 workers have some form of RSI.

   Approximately 600,000 employees miss some work as a result of RSI.

   Using a keyboard or mouse for more than four hours a day is considered a risk factor for RSI.

   Prevention programs could eliminate 460,000 injuries every year.

3. Say **SELECT A Growing Problem** and say • **CAP THAT** • **BOLD THAT** • **ITALICIZE THAT** to format this subtitle.

4. Say **SELECT Repetitive stress injury THROUGH year period.** (This will select all the lines that will be bulleted)

5. Say • **BULLET THAT**

Of the 257 respondents, 70 employees reported RSI symptoms. Of those, 27 or 10.5% were classified with carpal tunnel syndrome, which is similar to that found in the general population in past studies.

A Growing Problem

Repetitive Stress Injury (also known as RSI) has become a major problem. Many professionals are now at risk for RSI. For example:

- An estimated 25% of computer users will suffer some form of RSI during their careers.
- Over 1,800,000 workers have some form of RSI.
- Approximately 600,000 employees miss some work as a result of RSI.
- Using a keyboard or mouse for more than four hours a day is considered a risk factor for RSI.
- Prevention programs could eliminate 460,000 injuries every year.

*Hint: To turn bullets off, select the line you do not want bulleted and say **UNBULLET THAT***

6. **Say SAVE DOCUMENT** to update your file **Chapter 8 Preventing Computer Injuries**.

8.6 Inserting

Note when using the INSERT BEFORE and INSERT AFTER commands, you may need to scroll up or down to be sure you can see the text where you are wanting the cursor to move to.

1. Be sure your **Chapter 8 Preventing Computer Injuries** is Open.

2. Add to the Mayo Clinic Study heading.

3. Say **INSERT AFTER Mayo Clinic Study** and say **on June 12, 2001 reported:**

4. Insert your name after the title. Say:

    INSERT AFTER *PREVENTING COMPUTER INJURIES*

5. Say • **NEW PARAGRAPH** to create a couple of spaces.

6. Dictate **Your Name.** (Note: Bold your name if it did not automatically bold.)

    Say • **NEW PARAGRAPH**

7. Insert today's date

    SAY **Insert DATE AND TIME** (*The Date and Time Dialog Box will appear*) Say move down 2 (or desired #) to pick Month Day, Year format, Say OK

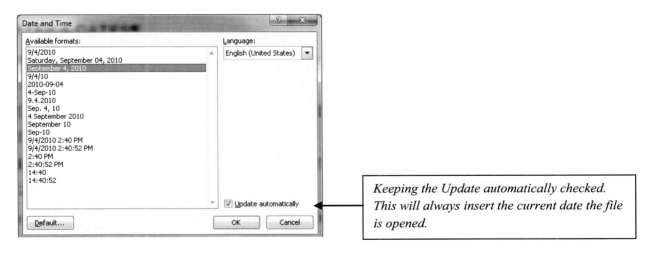

Keeping the Update automatically checked. This will always insert the current date the file is opened.

PREVENTING COMPUTER INJURIES

Your Name

October 3, 2008

For April, Miguel, and Maria, the pains of repetitive stress injury came early in life. (The names have been changed to protect privacy.) For this trio, symptoms began in their elementary typing classes. By the time they reached the required middle school typing class, their pains were getting worse.

Mayo Clinic Study on June 12, 2001 reported:

As people get older, a greater percentage of the population is impacted by repetitive stress injuries. In a recent study at the Mayo Clinic in Scottsdale, Arizona, 29.6% of hospital respondents reported numbness, prickly sensations or abnormal sensitivity.

Of the 257 respondents, 70 employees reported RSI symptoms. Of those, 27 or 10.5%

8.7 Cut That, Copy That and Paste That

COPY THAT – copies selected text
CUT THAT – cuts the selected text (removes it from the document)
PASTE THAT – inserts the copied or cut text into the document where cursor is

1. Dictate the following passage and then follow the steps below to practice the cut, copy and paste commands above. Say **NEW LINE** after each sentence.

   You will soon be flying through your documents with voice commands making the necessary changes.
   Keep practicing!
   Do not be discouraged if you do not remember all the voice commands at first.
   Learning formatting commands takes time and practice.

2. Say **SELECT Keep practicing exclamation mark**, say **CUT THAT**

3. Say **GO TO TOP** (moves cursor to beginning of first sentence), say **PASTE THAT**

4. Say **SELECT Learning THROUGH practice period**, say **CUT THAT**

5. Say **INSERT BEFORE You will**, say **PASTE THAT**

6. Say **SELECT Do not be THROUGH at first period**, say **CUT THAT**

7. Say **INSERT BEFORE You will**, say **PASTE THAT**

8. Say **SELECT Keep practicing exclamation mark**, say **COPY THAT**

9. Say **GO TO END OF PARAGRAPH**, say **PASTE THAT**

10. The final paragraph should read as follows:

    Keep practicing! Learning formatting commands takes time and practice. Do not be discouraged if you do not remember all the voice commands at first. You will soon be flying through your documents with voice commands making the necessary changes. Keep practicing!

11. Save the document as: 8.7 cut copy paste

8.8 Aligning Text and Changing Font

1. Be sure your **Chapter 8 Preventing Computer Injuries** is Open.

2. Select the title **PREVENTING COMPUTER INJURIES** with your voice.

3. Say • **CENTER THAT** to center the title.

4. Select your name with your voice.

5. Say • **CENTER THAT** to center your name.

6. Select the date with your voice.

7. Say • **FORMAT THAT CENTERED** to center the date.

8. Select the subtitle **A Growing Problem** with your voice.

9. Say • **RIGHT ALIGN THAT** to shift the subtitle to the right margin of the page.

10. Select the subtitle **Mayo Clinic Study on June 12, 2001 Reported:** with your voice.

11. Say • **FORMAT THAT RIGHT ALIGNED** to shift the subtitle to the right margin of the page.

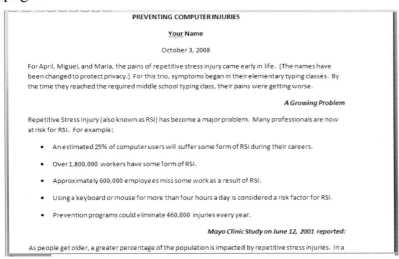

12. Select the subtitle **A Growing Problem** with your voice.

13. Say • **LEFT ALIGN THAT** to shift the subtitle to the left margin of the page.

14. Select the subtitle **Mayo Clinic Study on June 12, 2001 Reported:** with your voice.

15. Say • **FORMAT THAT LEFT ALIGNED** to shift the subtitle to the left margin of the page.

16. Say • **SELECT ALL** to select the entire document.

17. Say• **FORMAT THAT 18 (POINTS)** to change the font size to 18 points.

> **Puzzled?** Command words in (parenthesis) are optional. You don't need to say them if you don't want to.

18. Say • **GO TO TOP** to move to the beginning of the document to view the changes

19. Say • **SELECT ALL** to select the entire document.

20. Say • **FORMAT THAT 10 (POINTS)** to change the font size to 10 points

21. Say • **GO TO TOP** to move to the beginning of the document to view the changes

22. Say • **SELECT ALL** to select the entire document

23. Say • **FORMAT THAT 14 (POINTS)** to change the font size to 14 points.

24. Say • **GO TO TOP** to move to the beginning of the document to view the changes.

25. Say • **SELECT ALL.**

26. Say • **FORMAT THAT ARIAL** to change the font to Arial. Then say • **GO TO TOP** to move to the beginning of the document to view the changes.

27. **Say SELECT ALL, FORMAT THAT TIMES**

28. Using the • **SELECT PARAGRAPH** or • **SELECT LINE** commands, change the font size and style of your document in the following way:

   • Make the main title **Arial, 18 Points, Bold**

   • Make your name **Arial, 14 Points**

   • Make the date **Times, 14 Points**

   • Make the subheadings **Arial, 14 Points, Bold**

29. **Practice changing the text color with** • **MAKE THAT "COLOR"**

   • Select any paragraph or title and **MAKE THAT RED**

   • Select another paragraph or title and say • **MAKE THAT BLUE** to turn the paragraph text color to blue.

   • Select a third paragraph or title and say • **MAKE THAT GREEN** to turn the paragraph text color to green.

   • Select the entire document and restore the text color to black by saying • **MAKE THAT BLACK.**

30. Compare your document with this example and make any corrections needed. **Say "SAVE DOCUMENT"** to update your file **Chapter 8 Preventing Computer Injuries** .

PREVENTING COMPUTER INJURIES

Your Name

October 3, 2008

For April, Miguel, and Maria, the pains of repetitive stress injury came early in life. (The names have been changed to protect privacy.) For this trio, symptoms began in their elementary typing classes. By the time they reached the required middle school typing class, their pains were getting worse.

A Growing Problem

Repetitive Stress Injury (also known as RSI) has become a major problem. Many professionals are now at risk for RSI. For example:

   • An estimated 25% of computer users will suffer some form of RSI during their careers.

   • Over 1,800,000 workers have some form of RSI.

   • Approximately 600,000 employees miss some work as a result of RSI.

   • Using a keyboard or mouse for more than four hours a day is considered a risk factor for RSI.

   • Prevention programs could eliminate 460,000 injuries every year.

8.9 Format Spacing

1. Be sure your **Chapter 8 Preventing Computer Injuries** is Open.

2. Say • **INSERT BEFORE For April** to move to the first paragraph.

3. Say • **TAB KEY or • PRESS TAB** to indent the first line a default of ½ inch.

4. Say • **TAB KEY or • PRESS TAB** to tab the remaining paragraphs in the document that are unbulleted.

5. Move down to each of the three tabbed paragraphs and double space them by saying:
    *   **SELECT PARAGRAPH**
    *   **DOUBLE SPACE THAT**

6. Compare your document with the picture below and Say • **SAVE** to update your file.

7. Say **Print the File** and notice the print dialog box will appear. Check settings and say **OK**.

8.10 Dictate, Edit and Format Report "The Nature of Voice-Writing"

1. Turn on your Microphone and open Microsoft Word to create a new document.

2. Dictate the following paragraphs (Say **Tab Key** to indent paragraphs and **New Line** at the end of each paragraph)

> **People have the ability to carry on conversations and tell stories. Almost everyone can relate to a story and say something meaningful. And now they have the software to turn their speech into writing.**
>
> **Voice-writing requires practice and lots of it. People adjust the pace of their writing to the efficiency of their input tools. In centuries past, writers would saddle their thoughts and slow them down to a walk when crafting paragraphs with pen and ink. Eventually, writers learned to type and entered their thoughts into typing machines at a trot, or even a gallop, to the rhythmic tapping of their fingers across the keyboard. By comparison, voice-writers produce copy at a run. Learning to think, compose, speak clearly, and edit at the speed of speech takes effort and rehearsal.**
>
> **Inefficient keyboarding can retard the flow of ideas. It often causes writers, young writers in particular, to forget much of what they wish to communicate. Many potentially talented writers are intimidated or inhibited by their input tools. Inefficient typists, or those with poor penmanship, often shy away from the written craft. Poor scholars hesitate to write for fear that misspelled words will show them up.**
>
> **But writing isn't spelling, typing, or penmanship. Writing is the artful communication of ideas in a written form. Speech recognition has made it possible for anyone who can think and speak clearly to write clearly as well. Inadequate spelling, erratic typing, or poor penmanship are no longer barriers to written expression. Writing can now become a process of thinking and expressing, supported by careful proof-reading and thoughtful editing.**

3. Use the **"Play that Back"** or **"Read that"** commands to help you proofread. Correct each and every mistake in the three paragraphs above using the **SELECT** and **CHOOSE**, **SELECT and SAY** or **SPELL THAT** commands.

4. **Go to Top**, to add the title Say THE NATURE OF VOICE-WRITING (**ALL CAP THAT, BOLD THAT**) NEW LINE

5. Say Copyright sign, speaking solutions, 2010 **CAP THAT** (if line appears bolded say "restore that" to turn off bolding" **NEW LINE**

6. Say **Select all**, Say **Double Space that**

7. Say **Center the first two lines**

8. Compare your document to the sample on the next page and make any corrections.

9. Say "**Save Document AS**", with the cursor in the filename box, Say "**Chapter 8 The Nature of Voice-Writing**".

10. Say **Print the File**. Check settings and say **OK**.

THE NATURE OF VOICE WRITING

©Speaking Solutions 2001

People have the ability to carry on conversations and tell stories. Almost everyone can relate to a story and say something meaningful. And now they have the software to turn their speech into writing.

Voice-writing requires practice and lots of it. People adjust the pace of their writing to the efficiency of their input tools. In centuries past, writers would saddle their thoughts and slow them down to a walk when crafting paragraphs with pen and ink. Eventually, writers learned to type and entered their thoughts into typing machines at a trot, or even a gallop, to the rhythmic tapping of their fingers across the keyboard. By comparison, voice-writers produce copy at a run. Learning to think, compose, speak clearly, and edit at the speed of speech takes effort and rehearsal.

Inefficient keyboarding can retard the flow of ideas. It often causes writers, young writers in particular, to forget much of what they wish to communicate. Many potentially talented writers are intimidated or inhibited by their input tools. Inefficient typists, or those with poor penmanship, often shy away from the written craft. Poor scholars hesitate to write for fear that misspelled words will show them up.

But writing isn't spelling, typing, or penmanship. Writing is the artful communication of ideas in a written form. Speech recognition has made it possible for anyone who can think and speak clearly to write clearly as well. Inadequate spelling, erratic typing, or poor penmanship are no longer barriers to written expression. Writing can now become a process of thinking and expressing, supported by careful proof-reading and thoughtful editing.

This chapter gave you practice dictating, editing and formatting reports using Microsoft Word. Additional exercises are included in the REINFORCEMENT ACTIVITIES section in the back of the book.

CHAPTER 9—WEB NAVIGATION/SEARCHES, VOICE SHORTCUTS, & E-MAILS

Dragon makes it easy to navigate the internet, conduct searches, and use e-mail programs. Shortcuts for Web Search allow you to search the internet using commands that are patterned on your natural speech. Your web browser does not have to be open when you use these commands: You can use Dragon to read, write, send, and receive e-mail in many e-mail applications. (Before you start, remember that even though you can do everything by voice, many people find it more efficient to use a combination of mouse, keyboard, and dictation).

9.1 Web Search Shortcuts

Look at the following chart and try the examples yourself. You may also want to try coming up with some of your own searches.

Shortcut Type	Example command	What happens
Search the web for <dictation>	"Search the web for Italian restaurants in Phoenix"	Your default web browser opens and displays the results of a search on the phrase "Italian restaurants in Phoenix".
Search <website> for <dictation>	"Search eBay for Big Screen TV's"	Your default web browser opens and displays the results of searching eBay for the phrase "Big Screen TV's". You can search eBay, Amazon, Google, Yahoo, and more. See the online help for information on supported sites.
Find a website about <dictation>	"Find a site about alternative energy"	Your default web browser opens and displays Google's top-ranked page for the phrase "alternative energy" using Google's search
Search <category> for <dictation>	"Search video for World War II"	Your default web browser opens and displays the results of a search on the phrase "World War II" in your default search engine's video

9.2   Navigating the Internet

- To start Internet Explorer, you can either say "Start Internet Explorer" or you can simply click the Internet Explorer icon on your desktop. To start Firefox, you can either say "Start Mozilla Firefox" or you can simply click the FireFox icon on your desktop.

- You can say web addresses as you normally speak them. For example, to dictate "http://www.nuance.com/dragon", say "http www dot nuance dot com slash dragon"

- You can say the following abbreviations by pronouncing them as words: com, gov, mil, net, org, and sys.

- You must say "Click" before the name of the hyperlink.

- When navigating the internet, it is best to pause after each command and wait until it is completed before giving another command.

The following exercise gives you practice navigating the Internet. Be sure to say the full commands in [ ]

[Start Internet Explorer] (*wait for program to completely load*)

[Go to Address] Say: www.nuance.com

[Go there]

[Click Company] (this selects and opens the company page)

 [Scroll down]

[Click Leadership Team]

 [Move down 6]

[Go to Top]

[Go to Bottom]

[Scroll up]

[Go Back]

[Go Forward]

[Go Home] (*Takes you to home page*)

[Go to Address]

Say: google.com [Go there]

Say: NASA space shuttle (in the Google search box)

[Press Enter]

 [Go home]

- You can also use the "Search <site> for <xyz> command to launch searches on many Web Sites, including Facebook, Twitter, Bing,

- Your web browser does not have to be open to start a web search by voice. Dragon recognizes when you use a voice search command and opens the default browser for you.

Use the Dragon Sidebar for Internet Explorer to try some of your own internet commands.

9.3 Using E-mail

Using Dragon NaturallySpeaking to dictate e-mail messages follows the same dictation basics, correction techniques and formatting commands that you used to create other documents.

Dragon has many built in commands for Microsoft Outlook, Lotus Notes, Mozilla Thunderbird, Windows Mail, Windows Live Mail and Gmail (in supported web browsers). It also works with most other e-mail programs but each e-mail system may be slightly different. **Here is a list of common e-mail commands.**

To...	Say...
Start the default email program	START MAIL
Check for new messages	CHECK FOR MAIL
Open the selected message	OPEN MAIL
Close the selected message	CLOSE MAIL
Create a message	NEW MAIL
Send a message	SEND MAIL
Forwards the selected or open message	FORWARD MAIL
Replies to the selected or open message	REPLY TO MAIL
Deletes the selected or open message	DELETE MAIL

As you create messages, you can use the following commands:

- Go to To Field" – moves the cursor to the To: field so that you can then dictate the recipient's address.
- "Go to CC Field" - moves the cursor to the CC: field.
- "Go to Subject Field" - moves to cursor to the Subject field so that you can then dictate the subject.
- "Go to Body Field" – moves the cursor to the body of the e-mail so that you can dictate the message.
- You can also say TAB KEY to move down to the next field.

You can also use the Dragon Help menu to search for many helpful Email Program tips.

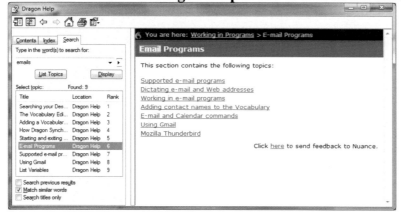

9.4   E-mail Exercise

Say: Start Microsoft Outlook <u>or</u> (e-mail program of your choice) and try the following exercise:

- [NEW MESSAGE] Say: bob no space jones @yahoo.com (Do not worry about capitalization here)
- [Go to Subject Field] sample e-mail CAP THAT
- [Go to Body Field] Say: This is a sample e-mail. You can talk and Dragon NaturallySpeaking will write what you say.

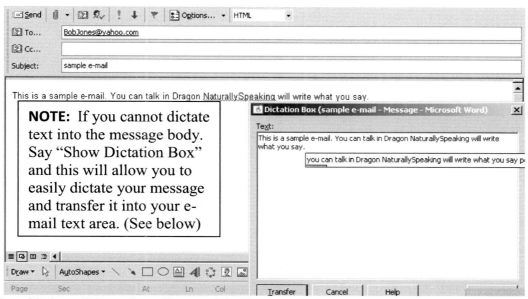

9.5   Using Dictation Box with Email

Remember, you may occasionally find an application or a specific window where some voice commands won't work or will not work consistently. This often happens with e-mail programs and industry-specific software.

Dragon may open the Dictation Box automatically or you can use the **SHOW DICTATION BOX** command to open the Dictation box. (This will allow you to use your voice to dictate, edit and transfer information into the desired application).

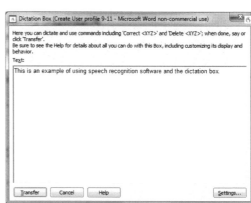

- At the end of your e-mail message in Activity 9.4, say NEW PARAGRAPH.
- Say: SHOW DICTATION BOX (or click Tools, Dictation Box on the DragonBar)
- When the Dictation Box appears, say: **This is an example of using speech recognition in the dictation box.**
- Practice select-and-say feature. Say: **SELECT using speech recognition in**
- While it is selected, replace that text by saying: **dictating text into**
- Say: **TRANSFER** *(closes dictation box and text is entered at location of cursor in application)*
- CLICK CLOSE to exit the e-mail program.

CHAPTER 10—ENHANCING YOUR PROFILE

There are many ways that you can improve your overall accuracy and enhance your speech recognition profile. You have already learned how to add and train words with the Vocabulary Editor and have been using the CORRECT and SPELL THAT commands. Dragon NaturallySpeaking has many other tools that will help you customize your vocabulary, add and train words quickly, and make custom commands and shortcuts. Review the information in 10.1 before doing the activities in 10.3.

10.1 Customizing your Vocabulary

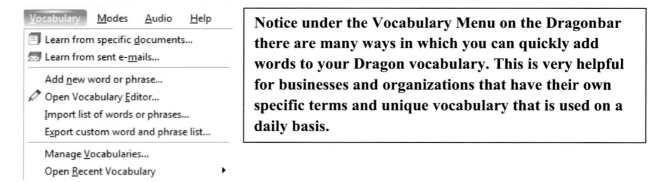

Notice under the Vocabulary Menu on the Dragonbar there are many ways in which you can quickly add words to your Dragon vocabulary. This is very helpful for businesses and organizations that have their own specific terms and unique vocabulary that is used on a daily basis.

Add new word or phrase — is used when you come across a unique word or phrase and want to add it to your vocabulary. Phrases are often added to keep specific capitalization/formatting. Example: Skyline High School instead of Skyline high school.

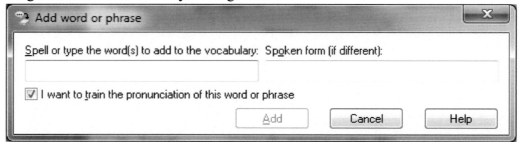

This was introduced with the "Vocabulary Editor" in Chapter 6, Page 47.

Learn from specific Documents—is a quick way to have Dragon analyzes your chosen documents to add any unrecognized words to your vocabulary all at once. Following are the steps you would take to analyze specific documents and add any unrecognized words to your vocabulary all at once.

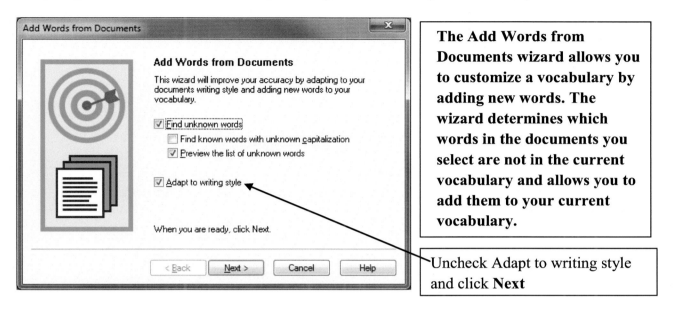

The Add Words from Documents wizard allows you to customize a vocabulary by adding new words. The wizard determines which words in the documents you select are not in the current vocabulary and allows you to add them to your current vocabulary.

Uncheck Adapt to writing style and click **Next**

Click on **Add Folder** and **Browse** for the folder that has your files. (In this example, the folder is called Medical Cases and we are including the whole folder). Click **OK** and a list of documents will appear in the next box.

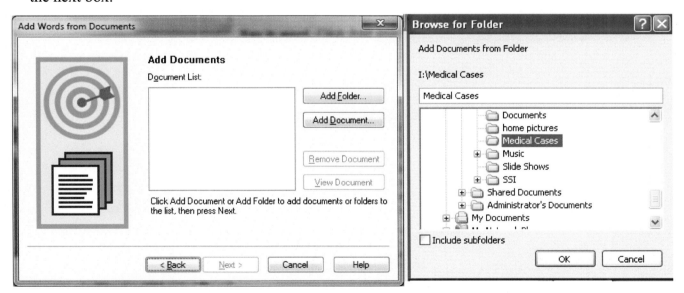

Click **Next** to analyze documents

Click **Next** when analysis is complete

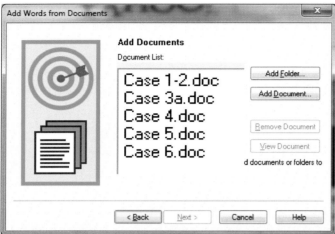

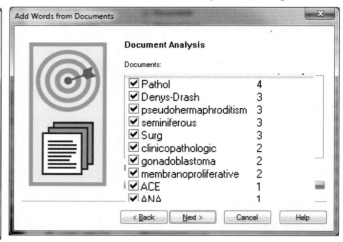

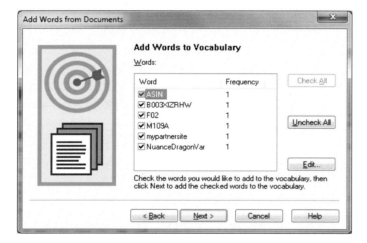

A list of words will show with the number of times they have appeared in the documents. Keep the words checked that you want added to your vocabulary.

(A message saying "No New Words Were Found" indicates all words are already in your vocabulary.).

Click **Next** to Continue

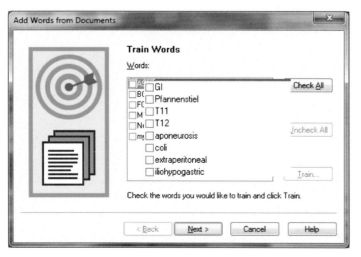

You can train the pronunciation of any word by checking the box next to the word and clicking Train. This can be done here <u>OR</u> at a later time.

Click **Next** to finish

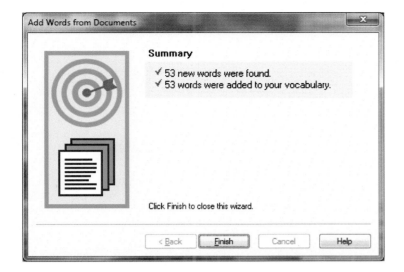

The last box gives you a summary of how many new words were added.

10.2 Create a List of Words to Add

If you don't have words already in a document to analyze, you can prepare a list of words to add and save the list as a .txt document. The document with the list of words would then be added to your vocabulary by following the same steps for adding words from a document and choosing the list name. Review the following steps before doing the activity in 10.3.

1. Create a document for the new words. You can use <u>any</u> word processor to create the document as long as you can save the final version as a text (.TXT) file.

2. Enter each word on a separate line. Make sure words are spelled correctly and there are <u>no</u> bullets or special formatting included. The list can include multiple-word phrases and spoken forms for words.

    To add a multiple-word phrase, such as "Mayberry Tribune," enter it on one line.

    To include a spoken form for a word, type the word followed by a backslash (\) and the spoken form. For example, to have Dragon enter "Robert F. Kennedy" when you say "RFK" type: Robert F. Kennedy\RFK

> Terms
> Phrases
> Mayberry Tribune
> Robert F. Kennedy\RFK

3. You may want to create a folder for storing all the word lists you create. This sample has a new folder called Dragon Word List.

Click New Folder Icon to Create Folder

4. Be sure to choose **Save As Type** and save as a text (.TXT) file

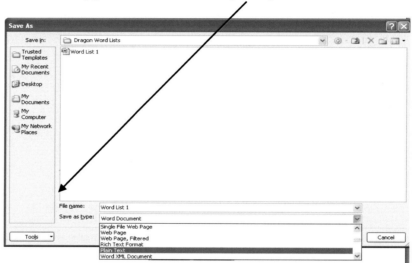

10.3 Practice Adding Words to Your Own Profile

- <u>Learn from Specific Documents</u>: Look at what files and folders you have saved on your computer or network location. Say SWITCH TO DRAGONBAR, VOCABULARY, LEARN FROM SPECIFIC DOCUMENTS (or use mouse to click Vocabulary, Learn from specific documents)

- <u>Create a Word List and add words to profile</u>: Start with these unique movie words and add more of your own. Such as names of school organizations, first & last name of friends or relatives.

  > "Sweet Jenkies"
  > "Jumpin Jahoesaphat"
  > "Pigalahootin"
  > "Jiminy Cricket"

- Follow the steps above to save your list in plain text format as **mylist.txt**

- Add your list of words to your vocabulary by following the steps in 10.1 steps "Learn from Specific Documents"

10.4   Create a Custom Command (MACRO)

You can easily create your own commands or shortcuts to save you time as you dictate. These voice commands are popular for addresses, signature blocks, and sections of text that are often repeated. Graphics can also be included in custom commands. There are two popular ways to create these:

Add New Command
1.   Say: **ADD NEW COMMAND** (Or click Tools, Add New Command on the DragonBar)
2.   In the My Command Name box, say or type INSERT SPEAKING SOLUTIONS ADDRESS, ALL CAP THAT. (Note: make sure the name is at least two words; making the word "insert" part of the name avoids naming it something that you may want to dictate as text later.)
3.   In the Content window, type or dictate the following:

     Speaking Solutions, Inc.

     2445 Lake Shore Drive

     Union, NE 68455
4.   Check the **Plain Text** box so the command will be entered in the same font style and size as the text preceding it in the document.
5.   Click **Train** to train the command; Click **Save** to save it in your profile.
6.   Try the command in a clear Microsoft Word document.

Make That a Shortcut
1.   In Microsoft Word, dictate or key the following:

     Madison High School

     345 Tiger Lane

     Madison, TN 37115
2.   Say: **SELECT ALL**
3.   Say: **MAKE THAT A SHORTCUT** (The MyCommands Editor will open with the selected text in the Content area and the cursor in the MyCommands Name box.)
4.   Say: **INSERT SCHOOL ADDRESS**, Say **CAP THAT**
5.   Check Say **PLAIN TEXT** (or use mouse) to check the box in front of Plain Text
6.   **Train** and **Save** the custom command as described in the Add New Command activity above.
7.   Try the new command in Microsoft Word.

Take time to add some of your own custom commands/shortcuts…home address, signature block, school or company address, etc…

10.5 Viewing and Editing Commands

The **Command Browser** is a window where you can locate voice commands that Dragon recognizes, including commands that are provided with the software as well as any commands that you or your system administrator might have added (custom commands). The **Command Browser** is the most comprehensive place to see the commands that are available in each application. You can also use the Command Browser to: view, create, train and edit commands

Say OPEN COMMAND BROWSER or go to Tools menu, and choose Command Browser.

> **Click** on the **Script** mode
>
> This mode allows you to delete, edit, copy, or preview any of your custom commands.

> Notice any command that you have added will have an $\cdot\text{-}^{A}\text{B}$ Symbol in front of the command

> Click on $\cdot\text{-}^{A}\text{B}$ Insert Speaking Solutions and click on **edit.** Notice the My commands Editor box opens.

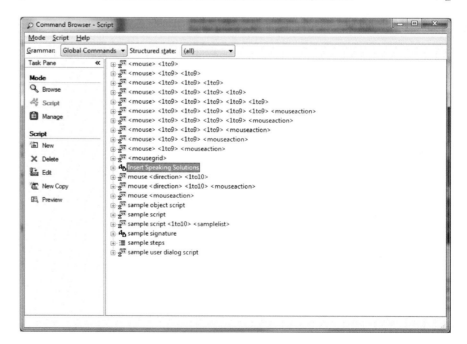

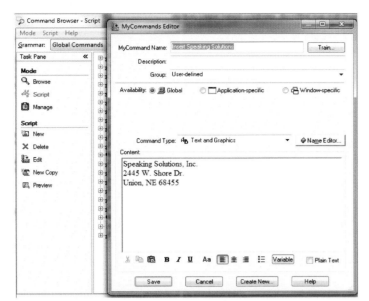

Edit this command by changing Speaking Solutions, Inc. to Speaking Solutions Foundation and Click SAVE

Remember you can delete, edit, preview or copy any of the commands you created here.

10.6 Create a Command including a Block of Text and Graphic

- **Open a new document in Microsoft Word**

- **Dictate** the following Preamble (don't forget to dictate all punctuation.)

> **We the people of the United States, in order to form a more perfect union, establish justice, insure domestic tranquility, provide for the common defense, promote the general welfare, and secure the blessings of liberty to ourselves and our posterity, do ordain and establish this Constitution for the United States of America. (New Paragraph)**

- Say **Click insert. Click Clip Art** (or use your mouse to go to Insert menu and choose Clip Art)

- Use your mouse to search for and select an American flag graphic to place it in the document. Resize it to about one inch.

- Say **CENTER THAT** to center the flag below the paragraph

- Proofread, correct and train any errors.

- Say **SELECT ALL** to select entire paragraph and flag graphic, Say **MAKE THAT A SHORTCUT.**

- Name your shortcut command **INSERT PREAMBLE, Click Train** and **Click Save.**

- Test your command by saying **INSERT PREAMBLE,** the entire paragraph and flag should appear on your screen.

10.7 Using The Accuracy Center and Dragon Help

The accuracy center is a central location for a variety of features that helps you increase your overall accuracy. You have used many of these features throughout this book. You can say OPEN ACCURACY CENTER or choose Improve my accuracy under the help menu.

Dragon Naturally Speaking also has an excellent help menu built into the software. You can quickly search numerous topics and get step-by-step directions by saying GIVE ME HELP or choosing Help Topics, under the Help menu.

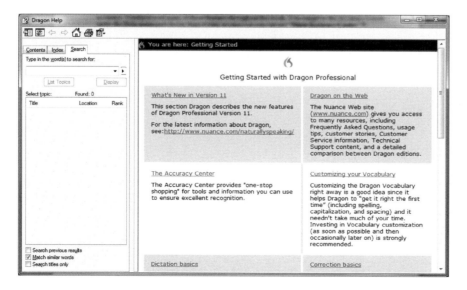

CHAPTER 11—REINFORCEMENT ACTIVITIES

You should now have a good basic understanding of how to use Dragon NaturallySpeaking to dictate, edit, correct, train and format text. Remember, speech recognition is just an additional inputting tool. Depending on the project, sometimes the keyboard or mouse is the best tool for the task. However, speech recognition is generally the best tool for inputting large amounts of text quickly. Do not get discouraged if you are not proficient at speech recognition immediately. Learning a new skill takes time and requires practice.

The following activities will help you reinforce your speech recognition skills as you use a variety of programs to create a mixture of documents. You can use Dragon NaturallySpeaking basic dictation techniques and commands with almost all other software programs. E-mail and word processing programs are the most popular because they are the most text intensive. However, voice-input can save time with many other applications. Remember, you can say "SHOW DRAGON SIDEBAR" or "GIVE ME HELP" to review tips and a list of commands for the program you are using.

Activity 1: Creating an email message
Create the following email message. You can use your e-mail program OR just dictate this message in Word. Think about your attack strategies before you begin. For example, you may wish to add and train Lake WaConDa; a unique two-word location. Don't forget to use your custom command at the bottom of the memo to enter the Speaking Solutions address.

> **At 10:35 PM last evening, our business office in Lake WaConDa was hit by a tornado. Our tornado was one of seven to hit Union County in 24 hours. Businesses on both sides of our administrative center were damaged extensively. A building to the south was completely destroyed. Office supplies were found 200 feet away in a nearby field. A large tree branch was driven through the roof of the office complex next door. Fortunately, no employees were working late in the evening, and no one was injured.**
>
> **Luckily, there was only minimal damage to the Speaking Solutions warehouse which stores hundreds of thousands of dollars of inventory and supplies. The accounting office suffered water damage as a result of the rain that came with the tornado.**
>
> **All electrical power and online services to the Home Office will be off for another 72 hours as repairs are made. Please use ground mail services for all communications for the next few days. Send all correspondence to:**
>
> **Speaking Solutions Foundation**
> **2445 Lake Shore Drive**
> **Union, NE 68455**

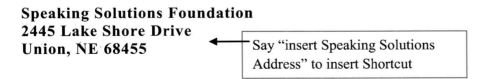 Say "insert Speaking Solutions Address" to insert Shortcut

Save document as: Speaking Solutions e-mail

Print

Activity 2: Creating Letters

Create the following letters using your voice. Think about your voice strategies. For example, don't forget to use the •INSERT DATE command to have the date at the top of the letters. Also dictate the city name, state name and zip code together. If you do so, Dragon NaturallySpeaking will format the state codes properly and automatically. In other words, Nebraska will turn into NE. **Proofread, edit, save and print each letter when you are done.**

Letter 1

- **START NEW DOCMENT**

  INSERT DATE *(Remember to move down to the date formatted with the month spelled out, day, and year.)*

  NEW PARAGRAPH
  NEW PARAGRAPH

  Dr. John Smith
  Jones Medical Center
  PO Box 52
  Big Springs, CO 50112 *(NEW PARAGRAPH)*

  Dear Dr. Smith *(NEW PARAGRAPH)*

  Dragon NaturallySpeaking is the top-selling speech recognition software on the market today. We are sure you will be very pleased with the performance of your new software. Our local University Medical Center has been using the software successfully to reduce costs and to increase efficiency. Medical reports are now prepared in a fraction of the time. We are sure you will experience the same results in your medical center. *(NEW PARAGRAPH)*

  Please feel free to contact us if you have any questions or would like additional training for your medical team. *(NEW PARAGRAPH)*

  Sincerely
  NEW PARAGRAPH
  NEW PARAGRAPH

  Joe Brown
  President and CEO

- Proofread and correct all errors including correct capitalization.

- **SAVE DOCMENT AS Letter 1**

LETTER 2

Insert your own information for the [ ] and use appropriate paragraph commands as in Letter 1

[Today's date]
Dear [FRIENDS NAME]

Many thanks for expressing an interest in my services. I realize there are numerous agents you might have chosen, so I greatly appreciate the opportunity to fulfill your insurance needs. I would consider it an honor and a privilege to work with you to achieve your business goals.

I am enclosing a packet of materials for you to review. Please note the highlighted text that addresses some of the concerns you shared.

Feel free to contact me anytime at [YOUR PHONE NUMBER], or visit my website at www.insuranceforyou.com if you have questions or need more information.

Sincerely

[YOUR NAME]
Insurance Agent

Enclosure

Save Document As Letter 2 *(remember to say numeral 2)*

LETTER 3

[Today's date]
Dear [FRIENDS NAME}

One of the best things about life insurance is the way that it offers something that is very hard to find: peace of mind.

Life insurance enables you to live your life to the fullest without worrying about whether or not your loved ones will have the financial security they need in the future. You will know with certainty that they will be cared for and protected from any future financial difficulties that may arise in your absence.

Financial security for one's family is an immense gift indeed--and it is more attainable than most people realize. The key to acquiring this success and financial security is to establish an excellent life insurance policy that is perfectly attuned to the needs of your family.

You deserve the peace of mind that a good policy can afford, and so do your loved ones. Why not visit my Website www.lifeinsuranceforyou.com or give me a call today at [YOUR PHONE NUMBER] to discuss your options? There is no obligation, but you may find it is a perfect fit for your needs.

[Closing of your choice]

Save Document As Letter 3

Activity 3: Creating Reports

Think of all the reports you have had to write over the years and the time you spent handwriting or keying them. Now think about the time you can save using voice-input. Think about your voice strategies as you complete the following two reports.

Report 1

Remember you may want to add and train proper names such as Ediphone in this report. Say • COPYRIGHT SIGN for ©. Use the •DOUBLE SPACE THAT command to double space entire report when done. Remember, if you are in double space mode, use the • NEW LINE command instead of • NEW PARAGRAPH so only one blank line appears between paragraphs.

Voice-Writing, Formatting and Editing
©Speaking Solutions Inc. 2012

Dragon NaturallySpeaking is a writer's tool. It allows composition without the physical constraints of a keyboard, mouse, pencil, or even a digital pen. Dragon allows your thoughts to verbally flow to the printed page.

Voice-writing is nothing new. In the 1940s a tool called the Ediphone was used by executives to dictate correspondence. Ediphone users described their work as **voice-writing.** It's an apt term. Since then, companies like Dictaphone and Sony have made dictation devices for busy doctors, lawyers, executives, and others too preoccupied (or unqualified) to do their own typing.

The popularity of voice-writing declined with the advent of the personal computer. An expectation grew during the 80s and 90s that everyone must learn to type their own written work. Typing became institutional. But the typing era is rapidly coming to a close as more efficient input tools are taught to a rapidly growing number of students, instructors, authors, and other professionals.

The Image of a Writer

A century ago, the image of a writer was a lone individual sitting at a rugged wooden desk with a quill pen, parchment, and a half-empty ink bottle. (Picture Jefferson penning his memorable letters to John Adams from his desk at Monticello.) In the late 1800s, the imagery changed. With the creation of the typewriter by Christopher Latham Scholes in 1867, what it meant to be a writer was increasingly identified by the act of typing. The lone author plying his or her trade at a typewriter or keyboard became emblematic of what it meant to be a writer. Just as an idyllic Jeffersonian image was abandoned, this imagery will inevitably change.

The depiction of writers at work today can portray entirely new stereotypes. Envision authors, journalists, or academics composing into mobile devices like iPhones or even smaller devices. They may be seen researching and voice-writing in the hallowed confines of a library — knowingly breaking the hushed silence. Writers can now combine digital pen input on smart screens with dictation. They may find themselves voice-writing while lounging at the beach, visiting a crime scene, investigating the site of a natural disaster, contemplating at a park, attending a press conference, or sitting alone at a local coffeehouse with their computer cradled like a clipboard.

The thought of a writer wandering the city streets or the countryside voice-writing and dictating notes on smart screens paints a radically new image of a writer. New advances in speech recognition and computer technology are quickly making this image a reality.

Be sure the report is double- spaced, proofread, edit and SAVE DOCUMEBNT AS Activity 3 Voice Writing Report.

Report 2

This was actually a newspaper article but can be formatted the same as a report. Glance through the report and add any unusual names of individuals or companies to your vocabulary before dictating. Remember, to dictate the retire report then use the "**Play that Back**" or "**Read that**" commands to help you proofread. Correct each and every mistake using the **SELECT** and **CHOOSE, SELECT and SAY** or **SPELL THAT** command and apply all formatting features.

Keep this report in BLOCK format. Single space paragraphs and double-space between paragraphs. (Use NEW PARAGRAPH instead of NEW LINE to do this). Bold the title and the side headings.

WITH TECH SKILLS, YOU CAN CONQUER THE WORLD (OR AT LEAST THE JOB MARKET) by Alex Foote
The Arizona Republic, Sunday, August 15, 2010

It's not always easy to master a new skill, especially a high-tech skill. But mastering technology skills can help you move forward in your career trajectory. People with cutting-edge high-tech skills always seem to find a job—even in the most hostile of job markets. That's because these individuals can do what others can't, and that makes them indispensable to employers.

How can you boost your technology skills to help you in the career search or job advancement? Here's what some career experts had to say:

Learn the Hottest Skills

All high-tech skills aren't created equal. You need skills that companies consider indispensable to their operations. For example, mobile-device skills are white hot. iPhones and their competitors have taken the high-tech world by storm, making the ability to develop applications, or apps, a priceless skill.

"People only exploit about 25 percent of the potential of the device," said Angela Fernando, tech column writer for *Communication World* magazine. "Just understanding how to maximize a piece of tech can help."

The Apple app store now has more than 185,000 apps, and companies are looking for people who can add more.

Master Search Engine Optimization

This is the practice of adjusting a website, through its coding or content, so that it appears as high as possible in the search engines results. The argument is that the higher a site is in their results, the more it will be clicked on.

Continue on next page

Report 2 Continued...

Start with a Book

When trying to learn high-tech skills, it can be easy to ignore the low-tech solutions. "If a person loves problem-solving and loves math, then picking up a book is a great way to get started," said Hamid Shojaee, CEO and founder of Axosoft, a Scottsdale-based software-development company.

The *Dummies* series is a great place for beginners with no experience to get their feet wet. You can start learning almost any programming language or any other technical skill this way.

Learn by Doing

Getting a high-tech job is more about your skills than formal training. "Formal education isn't something that is ultra-important to me," said J. Belfore, Partner and Systems Director of New Angle Media in Phoenix. "It's more important to have an impressive portfolio of work."

Teaching yourself these skills is a viable option for someone who doesn't have the time or the money for school.

"All of your education can be done on the computer," Belfore said, "The tools necessary to write programs are essentially free." Try to develop a fully functional project from the ground up, based on an imaginary company or real customer, if possible. This should get you an impressive portfolio and maybe a little money at the same time.

Don't Abandon Your Current Skills.

While having new skills can help open doors, it's important to not abandon skills considered standards.

"High-tech companies... want people that have good problem solving and good creativity," said Bassam Matar, engineering professor at Chandler-Gilbert Community College.

Communication is--and always will be--key. After all, what is the point of creating a high-tech project if you can't get the word out?

Be sure you proofread, edit and SAVE DOCUMENT AS Activity 3 Report 2.

Activity 4: Creating Tables

Tables are easy, convenient, and fun to create with Dragon NaturallySpeaking. After practicing several tables, you may come to feel that speech recognition is the best way to create and organize tables

Open Word and follow the steps below to create these two tables:

TABLE 1

1. Dictate the title: **The great northwest**
    - **UPPERCASE AND BOLD THAT**
    - **CENTER THAT**
2. **INSERT 2 BY 3 TABLE** (This will insert a table grid)
3. Be sure the cursor is in the first cell and dictate the following:

Idaho • **TAB**	1.7 million inhabitants • **TAB**
Oregon • **TAB**	5.3 million inhabitants • **TAB**
Washington • **TAB**	6.2 million inhabitants • **GO TO BOTTOM**

4. **SELECT IDAHO THROUGH 6.2 MILLION INHABITANTS, LEFT-ALIGN THAT**
5. **Save Document AS Table 1**

TABLE 2

1. Create a 3 x 5 table using the following natural command: **INSERT 3 BY 5 TABLE**
2. Move your insertion point to the first row and say:
    - **SELECT ROW** (may need to say Click Layout to be on the layout tab in 2007)
    - **CLICK MERGE CELLS**
3. With your insertion point still in the first row, say: college sports program
    - **UPPERCASE THIS ROW**
    - **BOLD THIS ROW**
    - **CENTER THAT**
4. Say • **PRESS TAB or TAB** to move the insertion point to the first cell in the second row
5. Say: **Fall events** • **TAB**   **Winter events** • **TAB**   **Spring events**
    - **SELECT ROW**
    - **CAPITALIZE THIS ROW**
    - **CENTER THIS ROW**
    - **BOLD THIS ROW**
6. Dictate the remaining words in the table as shown in this sample. Say • **TAB** to move the insertion point to the first cell in the third row or you can move the cursor by saying move up <1> row or move right <1> cell

COLLEGE SPORTS PROGRAM		
Fall Events	**Winter Events**	**Spring Events**
Football	Basketball	Golf
Soccer	Gymnastics	Baseball
Volleyball	Swimming	Softball

7. **Save Document AS Table 2**

Table Commands:
<n> = number

Insert a <n> x <n> table (Ex. Insert a 3 by 6 table)	opens the Table menu (If the command does not work, say *Click table, insert, table)*, say *numeral <n>* for columns, *tab-key, numeral <n>* for rows, OK
Select row or Select column	selects the row or the column the cursor is in
Add a row above/below or Insert <n> row(s)	inserts row or rows above where the cursor is located
Add a column to the left/right or Insert <n> columns	inserts column(s) to the left of where cursor is located
Delete row	removes row where cursor is
Delete column	removes column where cursor is
Press tab-key	moves cursor one cell to the right
Press Shift Tab	moves cursor one cell back
Move up/down <n>	moves cursor up or down specified number of cells
Move right/left <n>	moves cursor to right or left specified number of cells
Go to bottom	cursor leaves table and moves to line below table
Center that or Bold that	centers or bolds text, rows or columns *that has been selected*
Click Layout, AutoFit Contents	adjusts the table so the columns and rows fit the contents
Click Layout, AutoFit Window	Adjusts the table so the columns and rows fit from margin to margin
Click Layout, Merge Cells	merges selected cells into one cell
Click Layout, Properties, Center	aligns table center on the page

TABLE 3

Practice creating a table using the Table Commands above.

1. Open Microsoft Word to a new document.

2. Use voice commands to set font to Arial, 18 point (see Word commands in back of manual)

3. Create a 3 X 6 table like the illustration below.

4. Merge the first row and make the title 18 pt

5. You may want to dictate all information before formatting. (Remember to say **CAPS ON** before dictating the names or **CAP THAT** immediately following dictating the words or select later and say **CAP THAT**.

6. Bold and center the title and headings.

7. AutoFit the table to contents

8. If voice commands do not work appropriately in your version of Word, use mouse to click the menu items.

9. **Save Document AS Table 3**

Student Representatives		
Student	**School**	**School Phone**
John Anderson	Valley High School	673-455-0688
Karen Jones	Central High School	673-486-7832
Melinda Stephens	Appleton West High School	673-534-2376
Gary Bennett	Rockbridge High School	673-426-7832

Activity 5: Formatting Text Using Cut, Copy and Paste Commands

In a new document, complete the following activity using cut, copy, paste, capitalization, bold, italics, center, underline and other formatting commands. To review formatting commands, go to Chapters 7 and 8.

1. Set the font face to Arial and set the font size to 15.
2. Dictate the following sentences as written using the **NEW PARAGRAPH** command to separate the paragraphs. Use capitalization commands appropriately. Proofread and correct all misrecognized words before completing the exercises below.

One of the holes is called Temptation Corner, and another one is called Valley of Danger. One of my favorite golf courses is CEDAR CREEK GOLF CLUB in Branson, Missouri. It was designed by John Adams, local golf professional.

THE WORLD OF GOLF

This course has some challenging holes – even for the experienced golfer. It is the most beautiful course in Missouri. You may want to take some extra balls with you if you play this course.

Your First and Last Name

3. Use the cut, copy, center and paste voice commands to rearrange the above sentences into the paragraphs below. Format as directed below the paragraphs. Use your mouse to click the insertion points if you have trouble with the navigational commands. (Remember to use the **SELECT** **<beginning words> THROUGH <ending words>** to select an entire passage.

THE WORLD OF GOLF

One of my favorite golf courses is CEDAR CREEK GOLF CLUB in Branson, Missouri. It is the most beautiful course in Missouri. It was designed by John Adams, local golf professional.

This course has some challenging holes – even for the experienced golfer. One of the holes is called *Temptation Corner,* and another one is called *Valley of Danger.* You may want to take some extra balls with you if you play this course.

THE WORLD OF GOLF
By *Your Name*

4. Italicize Temptation Corner and Valley of Danger.
5. Center, Bold and Underline the title.
6. Save as: **Activity 5 world of golf**

Activity 6: Creating an Excel Spreadsheet

This activity will give you practice on using Dragon NaturallySpeaking with Microsoft Excel. You can use the Dragon Sidebar to look over the Excel commands and tips as needed. This activity gives you step-by-step directions to help you become familiar with what you can do by voice. In spreadsheets, many people find it faster to use the keyboard and mouse to TAB, ENTER or SELECT a cell. In this exercise, you can practice the voice commands, TAB KEY, PRESS ENTER, MOVE TO CELL <B6>, and decide which is more efficient for you.

Be aware that the software works slowly at first to analyze how you speak each new word/command, but gains speed as you repeat those same words/commands.

This is a preview of what your Excel spreadsheet should look like when you when you have completed all of the steps in this activity. Previewing your final result often helps you understand the steps better.

EXCEL 1

	A	B	C	D	E	F	G	H
1			Monthly Sales					
2			January	February	March	April	Total	
3			82	586	326	7000	7994	
4			67	637	387	9000	10091	
5			49	433	136	3500	4118	
6		Average	66	552	283	6500		
7								
8	California							
9	Florida							
10	Idaho							
11	Missouri							
12	Washington							
13		2001	2002	2003	2004	2005	2006	2007
14								
15	$12,690.00							
16	522.5625							
17	265							
18	159							
19								

1. START MICROSOFT (OFFICE) EXCEL (2003 or 2007)

2. Dictate the following: (Watch the screen to make sure each dictation or command is completed before dictating the next number or command.)

    82 **TAB**   586 • **TAB**   326 • **TAB**   7000 • **PRESS ENTER**

3. MOVE LEFT 3

4. Dictate the following:

    67 • **TAB**   637 • **TAB**   387 • **TAB**   9000 • **NEXT ROW**

5. MOVE LEFT 3

6. Dictate the following

    49 • **TAB**   433   • **TAB**   136 • **TAB**   3500 • **PRESS ENTER**

    (Continue on next page)

7. **PRESS CTRL HOME**
8. **INSERT 2 ROWS**
9. **MOVE RIGHT 1**
10. Say: Monthly Sales • **CAP THAT**
11. **MAKE THAT 15** • **PRESS ENTER**
12. **MOVE LEFT 1**
13. **INSERT 2 COLUMNS** • **DELETE COLUMN**
14. **SELECT COLUMN A THROUGH COLUMN H** *(or Select Column Alpha through Column Hotel)*
15. **SET COLUMN WIDTH TO 10**
16. **CELL B2** • **JANUARY THROUGH APRIL ACROSS**
17. **CAP** Total • **PRESS ENTER**
18. **CENTER ROW 2**
19. **MOVE TO CELL F 3** • **SUM THIS ROW**
20. **ADD UP THIS ROW** • **ADD UP THIS ROW**
21. **MOVE LEFT 5**
22. **CAP** Average
23. **PRESS TAB** • **AVERAGE THIS COLUMN**
24. **MOVE TO CELL B6** (or CELL BRAVO 6)
25. **COPY THAT**
26. **FILL CELL RIGHT 3 CELLS** (or Select Cell C6 through Cell E6 • Paste That)
27. **CELL A6** (or CELL ALPHA 6) This cell may already be selected.
28. **RIGHT ALIGN THIS CELL**
29. **BOLD COLUMN F**
30. **CELL A8** (or CELL ALPHA 8)
31. **THROUGH 15 DOWN**
32. **SELECT PREVIOUS 7 ROWS** • **CLEAR THAT**
33. **CELL A8** • **MOVE RIGHT 1**
34. **SUNDAY THROUGH SATURDAY ACROSS**
35. **CELL A 9** (or CELL A9)
36. **1 THROUGH 5 DOWN**
37. **CELL B8**
38. **2005 THROUGH 2011 ACROSS** (This will replace days of the week.)
39. **CELL F 8** • **UNBOLD THAT** (removes bold formatting)
40. **BEGINNING OF ROW** • **MOVE DOWN 1**
41. Washington **NEXT ROW**
42. Missouri **NEXT ROW**
43. California **NEXT ROW**

44. Florida **NEXT ROW**

45. Idaho **PRESS ENTER**

46. **SELECT CELL A9 THROUGH CELL A13**

47. **SORT THIS** (if dialog box appears, say "**Continue with current selection**," "**Sort**")

48. **CLICK OK** (to sort in ascending order) Note: In Word 2007, you must use your mouse to select the drop down menus to choose other sort options.

49. **CELL A15**

50. **MULTIPLY 846 TIMES 15**

51. **DIVIDE 8361 BY 16**

52. **SUBTRACT 82 FROM 347**

53. **ADD 86 PLUS 73**

54. (Answers to above four problems should be: 12690, 522.625, 265, 159)

55. **CELL A15 • CHANGE THIS TO CURRENCY WITH TWO DECIMALS** *(notice the change in format)* **CHANGE THIS TO GENERAL** *(notice the formatting changed back to General format)*

56. **SELECT CELL ALPHA 1 TO CELL HOTEL 19**

57. **SET BORDERS • CLICK INSIDE • CLICK OUTLINE • CLICK OK**

58. **PRESS CTRL HOME**

59. COMPARE YOUR SPREADSET TO THE SAMPLE ON Page 93.

60. PROOFREAD AND MAKE ALL CORRECTIONS

61. **SAVE DOCUMENT AS Activity 6 Excel 1**

EXCEL 2

- In a new Excel document, use the voice strategies you have learned to see how quickly you can create this simple spreadsheet by voice.

SCHOOL ENROLLMENT					
Grade level	2009	2010	2011	2012	TOTAL
Freshman	680	705	610	655	2650
Sophomore	610	650	715	590	2565
Junior	590	580	610	695	2475
Senior	610	560	550	575	2295

Use the SUM Function for the last column. Remember you can say "SUM UP THIS ROW" and "FILL CELL DOWN <3> CELLS"

- Proofread and make all corrections
- **SAVE DOCUMENT As** Activity 6 Excel 2

Activity 7:   Taking Notes and Conducting Research by Voice

Taking notes is easy with speech recognition software. Instead of highlighting your text as you read or take written notes, you can quickly dictate what you would highlight or write down. It is very easy to dictate exact passages and reference the page numbers for review later. Voice notes reinforce your reading comprehension and help you to create a summary of key points. In essence, your own quick study guides.

When conducting research, the Internet has become the research tool of choice for most people. Use your speech recognition software to help you navigate the web, organize your thoughts, take notes, keep track of your references and create a draft.

At first, you may feel a little uncomfortable talking to the computer, but after some practice, you'll find it easy and natural. The main thing is to speak naturally. Let the ideas flow from your brain to the screen. Speak your ideas as if you were answering a question for someone in person. This may help you overcome any awkward feelings that you have about talking to the computer.

Don't forget to turn off your microphone if you need some time to think or need to stop dictating for any reason. Remember the **RESUME WITH, INSERT BEFORE** and **INSERT AFTER** commands can be very helpful when composing with your voice. (See Page 64)

Taking notes for Report 2

Be sure you have completed the Activity 3 Report 2 document and have it printed for a hard copy reference. You will practice taking voice notes by answering questions about this article.

- First start a **New Document** and dictate "**These are my notes for Activity 3 Report 2 Article**" (NEW PRAGRAPH)

  (Look at the printout of the article to answer the following questions in complete sentences using your voice)

  1. What are the first two sentences under "Learn the hottest skills"?

  2. According to some career experts, what are the five ways you can boost your technology skills to help you in your career search or job advancement? (Hint: site headings in article, remember to use complete sentences).

  3. What quote in the article was stated by Hamid Shojaee, CEO and founder of Axosoft?

  4. What four things were quoted from J. Belfore, Partner and Systems Director of New Angle Media in Phoenix have the say?

- **SAVE DOCUMENT AS Notes for Report 2**

Activity 8 Using Voice Notations

Many people like to write comments or highlight text when they are editing documents. With Dragon NaturallySpeaking, you can make voice notations right into your document. To make a voice notation, hold down the escape key while you speak and the information that you dictate will be highlighted. Many people like to use this feature when they are revising drafts. Teachers love this feature for grading online papers.

Applying Voice Notations to Activity Report 2

Open your Activity Report 2 Document and add the following voice notations using the sample below.

- Say **Insert After indispensable to employers (period)**
- Hold down the **Esc** (Escape key) and say "**Do you have any cutting-edge high-tech skills?** Notice this sentence will appear highlighted, underlined and in different color text).
- Say **Insert Before boost your** and hold down the **Esc** (Escape key) and say **quickly**.
- Say **GO TO BOTTOM** hold down the **Esc** (Escape key) and say **This was an interesting article.**

Compare your **voice notations** with the sample below. You can try adding more of your own voice notations to this document for practice. **You do not need to save this activity.**

People with cutting-edge high-tech skills always seem to find a job, even the most hostile of job markets. That's because these individuals can do what others can't, and that makes them indispensable to employers. *Do you have any cutting-edge high-tech skills?*

How can you *quickly* boost your technology skills to help you in the career search or job advancement? Here's what some career experts had to say:

Communication is-and always will be-key. After all, what is the point of creating a high-tech project if you can't get the word out? *This was an interesting article.*

Use the tips, tricks, and strategies that you have learned throughout this training manual to continue to use and improve your speech recognition inputting skills on a daily basis.

COMMON DRAGON COMMANDS

<n> = number

Say . . .	To . . .
Microphone	
Stop Listening or Go to Sleep	Pauses the microphone *(listening but will not type)*
Listen to Me or Wake Up	Wakes microphone from pause
Microphone Off	Turns microphone off *(must be turned back on manually)*
Check Audio	Opens the wizard to check audio settings of the microphone
Navigation& Selection	
New Line or Press Enter	Press the Enter key once
New Paragraph	Press the Enter key twice
Press Space Bar	Insert a space
Tab Key, Press Tab Key or Tab	Press the Tab key
Go to Bottom	Move insertion point to end of document
Go to Top	Move insertion point to beginning of document
Beginning of Line or Beginning of Paragraph	Move insertion point to beginning or ending of current line or paragraph
End of Line or End of Paragraph	Move insertion point to end of current line or paragraph
Move left/right <n> characters/words	Move cursor left or right designated number of characters or words
Move up/down <n> lines/paragraphs	Move cursor up or down designated number of lines or paragraphs.
Insert Before<word or words> or Insert After <word or words>	Move insertion point before or after designated text to insert text there
Backspace or Press Backspace *(Can say Backspace 3, etc.)*	Erase one character/space to left of cursor or erases selected text and moves cursor one space left.
Press Delete	Erase one character/space to right of cursor
Select <specific words>, line, paragraph, all	Select specific words/lines/paragraphs/all to replace, correct, format, delete
Unselect That	Cancel selection
Select <word/words thru word/words>	Select phrase using first word or two through last word or two (Ex. "Select The box *thru* today period" to select the phrase "The box will be delivered to him today.")
Document Commands	***Document Commands***
Open new document or Close document	Open a new document or close the current document
Select <specific words>, line, paragraph, all	Select specific words/lines/paragraphs/all to replace, correct, format, delete
Start <program name>	Start <specific program>
Switch to <program name>	Switch to < another open program >
Save the document	Save the document
Clear document or Clear Page	Erase entire page
Add that as a Phrase	Add a repetitive phrase to vocabulary
Select <specific words>, line, paragraph, all	Select specific words/lines/paragraphs/all to replace, correct, format, delete

MICROSOFT WORD REFERENCE SHEET

Say . . .   To do this. . . .

Font Face, Size & Color

Say	To do this
Set font <font face>	Change font (Ex. Set font Times)
Format that <font face>	Change font face of SELECTED text
Set size <4-100>	Change font size (Ex. Set size 20)
Format that <font face><size>	Change font face and size (Ex. Format that Arial 15)
Make that <font face>	Change font on **selected** text
Make that <4-100>	Change font size on **selected** text
Make that <color>	Change font color of **selected** text (Ex. make that red)

Bold, Italics, Underline, Strikethrough

Say	To do this
Bold on, Italics on, Underline on	Turn on Bold, Italics or Underline enhancements
Bold off, Italics off, Underline off	Turn off Bold, Italics or Underline enhancements
Bold that, Italicize that, Underline that	Bold, italicize or underline **selected** text
Bold, italicize or underline the next (or this or previous) <n> words, lines, paragraphs	Bold, italicize or underline the current, next, or previous designated number of words, lines or paragraphs
Strikethrough this <word, line or paragraph>	Strikethrough the current word, line or paragraph
Strikethrough Off	Remove strikethrough from **selected** text
Restore that OR Format that regular	Remove bold, italics or underline from **selected** text
Bold (or Uppercase, Underline, Italicize or Underline) the <1st> paragraph	Performs specified enhancement on the designated paragraph

Tabs & Indents

Say	To do this
Show ruler or Hide ruler	Display ruler on page or Hide ruler on page
Tab Key or Press Tab Key or Tab	Tab to next position
Set left-align tab at <n> inches	Set left-align tab
Set center align tab at <n> inches	Set center tab
Set right-align tab at <n> inches	Set right-align tab
Clear the tab stop or clear tabs	Clear manually-set tab stops
Increase indent	Increase indent of document or selected paragraphs
Decrease indent	Decrease indent of document or selected paragraphs
Change the 1st line indent to <N> inch (ex. change the 1st line indent to .3 inches)	Change the indention point of the first line of all selected paragraphs in the document.
Indent this (line, paragraph, document)	Indent the designated text
Indent this (line, paragraph, document) by <n> inches (Ex. by point 7 inches)	Indent line, paragraph or document by specified number of inches.

Insert & Delete Lines

Say	To do this
Insert <n> lines	Insert designated number of blank lines at cursor
Delete previous <1-35> lines	Delete designated number of lines before cursor
Delete next <1-35> lines	Delete designated number of lines below cursor

Cut, Copy Paste

Say	To do this
Cut that, Copy that	Cut or Copy **selection** to clipboard
Paste that	Paste cut or copied text from clipboard

Bullets and Numbers

Say	To do this
Bullets on, Bullet that or Numbers on, Number that or Format that bullet style	Turn on bullets or numbers
Bullets off	Turn bullets off
Number that	Turn numbering on
Numbers off	Turn numbering off
Press Enter, Press Enter	Return cursor to left margin after a bulleted list

Capitalization	
Caps On OR Caps Off	Turn Capitalization on or off before dictating
All Caps On OR All Caps Off	Turn ALL CAPS (Uppercase) on or off
Uppercase that OR All Caps That	Change case of **selected** text to all uppercase
Capitalize that or Cap that	Capitalize the first letter of each word of the **selection**
No Cap that OR Lowercase that	Change case of **selected** text to lowercase
Capitalize this OR Capitalize next <n> words, line, paragraph, etc.	Capitalize designated words, lines, paragraphs, etc.
Uppercase this or Uppercase next <n> words, lines or paragraph, etc.	Change designated text to Uppercase
Lower case this or Lowercase next (or previous)<n> words, lines or paragraphs.	Change designated text to Lowercase
Alignment	
Center that, Left align that, Right align that, Justify that	Align the current paragraph or **selected** text
Right-Align, Left-Align, Center or Justify the <2nd> paragraph	Aligns the designated paragraph
Line Spacing	
Double space that OR Single space that	Set line spacing of current paragraph or **selected** text to double or single
Double space OR Single space the <next, third, first, etc.> paragraph	Set line spacing to double or single of designated paragraphs.
Double space OR Single space this document	Change line spacing of entire document
Set Margins	
Set left (right, top or bottom) margin to <1/2> inch	Change left, right, top or bottom margin to designated inches (Ex. set top margin to 2 inches)
Columns	
Change this (selection, paragraph, page or document) to <n> columns	Change text to designate number of columns
View	
Preview the file or Close Preview	Open Print Preview mode or Close Print Preview
Zoom to <N> Percent	Zoom to designated percentage (Ex. zoom to 75%)
Zoom to Whole Page	Zoom to full page view
Zoom to Page Width	
Miscellaneous	
Clear Document (or Page)	Delete all characters and images on screen
Find and Replace	Open find and replace box
Line <1-35>	Move cursor to the beginning of designated line on page
1st (or 2nd, 3rd, 4th, etc.) Paragraph	Move cursor to designated paragraph
Insert Page Break	Insert forced page break in document
Close Task pane	Close task pane if visible
Format that without spaces or compound that	Remove spaces from selected text (use Undo to restore)
Show/Hide Paragraph Marks	
Locate more formatting commands in the Command Browser under Tools.	

EXCEL COMMANDS REFERENCE SHEET

<N> = number   <L> = letter

Command	Action
Start the program:	
Start Microsoft Excel (or the name of program in the Start menu)	Launches the Excel program (program must be listed in the Start menu for this command to work)
Navigate the spreadsheet:	
Press Control Home or Go to Top	Moves cursor to Cell A1
Move up/down/right/left <N>	Moves cursor designated number of cells in designated direction
Beginning of Row	Moves cursor to beginning of row
Beginning of Column	Moves cursor to top of column
Move to Cell <LN> or Cell <LN>	Moves cursor to designated cell using regular or military alphabet (Ex. Move to Cell C3 or Move to Cell Charlie 3 or just say Cell C3)
Column <L>	Moves cursor to designated column (Ex. Column B or Column Bravo)
Row <N>	Moves cursor to designated row (Ex. Row 17)
Previous Row	Moves cursor up one row
Next Row	Moves cursor down one row
Previous Column	Moves cursor left one column
Next Column	Moves cursor right one column
Add rows, columns and worksheets:	
Insert <N> row(s)	Inserts row(s) above location of cursor
Insert column	Inserts one column to the left of cursor
Insert <N> column(s)	Inserts column(s) to left of cursor
Insert a new worksheet	Inserts a new worksheet
Select cells, rows, and columns:	
Select Cell <LN>	Selects designated cell (Ex. Select Cell D7)
Select Cell <LN> through Cell <LN>	Selects adjacent cells (Ex. Select Cell B2 through Cell D4)
Select Row	Selects current row
Select Row <N>	Selects designated row (Ex. Select Row 4)
Select Row <N> through Row <N>	Selects adjacent rows (EX. Select Row 2 through Row 8)
Select Column	Selects current column
Select Column <L>	Selects designated column (Ex. Select Column C)
Select previous/next <N> rows	Selects designated number of rows above or below active row
Select previous/next <N> columns	Selects designated number of columns to left/right of active column
Select all cells	Selects all cells in active portion of worksheet
Select the worksheet	Selects entire worksheet
Delete cells, rows, columns and worksheet:	
Delete cell(s)	Deletes selected cell(s) and opens dialog box to shift cells
Delete row	Deletes active row
Delete column	Deletes active column
Delete previous/next <N> rows	Deletes designated number of rows above active row
Delete previous/next <N> columns	Deletes designated number of columns to left of active column
Delete this worksheet	Deletes current worksheet
Erase contents:	
Clear that	Erases contents of selected cells, rows, columns or worksheet
Scratch that	Erases last dictation while still in cell
Clear all from this cell/row/column/sheet	Erases contents of designated cell/row/column/sheet
Insert Common Functions:	
Add up this row/column OR Sum this row/column	Inserts sum function and adds consecutive cells in row or column
Average this row/column	Averages consecutive cells in row or column
Average the values above	Averages consecutive cells in column
Insert Function	Opens Function dialog box (say "Select a Function" to activate list) (Ex. Insert function, Select a function, Move Down 2, OK, OK)

Say . . .	To do this. . . .
Perform mathematical equations:	
Multiply <N> times <N>	Multiplies dictated numbers (Ex. multiply 5,273 times 18)
Divide <N> by <N>	Divides first number by second number
Add <N> plus <N>	Adds dictated numbers
Subtract <N> from <N>	Subtracts first dictated number from second number
Insert consecutive months, days, numbers:	
<month> through <month> across/up/down/back	Enters months of the year in consecutive order in direction of command (Ex. January through April across)
<day> through <day> across/up/down/back	Enters days of the week in consecutive order in direction of command (Ex. Wednesday through Friday down)
<year> through <year> across/up/down/back	Enters years in consecutive or reverse consecutive order in direction of command (Ex. 2004 through 1999 up)
<N> through <N> across/up/down/back	Enters numbers in consecutive order in cells in direction designated (Ex. 50 through 60 across) Note: More than 20 consecutive numbers are written by 10s. Hundreds by hundreds. Thousands by thousands.
Align cells, rows and columns:	
Center that/Left align that/Right align that	Aligns the contents of the selected or active cells
Center this cell/row/column	Centers the contents in the designated cell/row/column
Left align this cell/row/column	Left aligns the contents in the designated cell/row/column
Right align this cell/row/column	Right aligns the contents in the designated cell/row/column
Edit Cells:	
Edit Cell <LN>	Allows navigational and formatting commands within the cell (Ex. move left 2, select-and-say, backspace 3, make that 15, etc.)
Edit cell or Press F2	Enters Quick Edit mode in designated cell to allow navigational and formatting commands within the cell
Apply	Applies editing changes and exits Quick Edit mode
Basic formatting:	
Set column width to <N>	Changes the width of selected columns to designated number
Bold That or Italicize That	Bolds or Italicizes contents of selected cells, rows or columns
Turn Bold/Italics/Underline On	Turns on bold/italics/underline feature
Turn Bold/Italics/Underline Off	Turns off bold/italics/underline feature
Format that Regular	Removes bold or italics from selected cells, rows or columns
Copy that	Copies selected cell, row, or column
Paste that	Pastes data from clipboard into selected cell, row or column
Format cell/row/column/worksheet	Opens Format Option dialog box (Ex. Format cell, Category, Move down 6, OK)
Sort selection, column:	
Sort this	Opens the Sort Menu to sort selection
Sort this column ascending/descending	Sorts numerical data in column in order commanded
Add borders:	
Set borders	Opens border dialog box, choose None, Inside or Outline borders for selected cells (Ex. Select all cells, Set borders, outline, inside, OK)
Remove border from this	Removes border from selected cell, row, column or worksheet
Add an inside *(or outside)* border to this worksheet OR Add an inside and outside border to this worksheet or selection	Adds an inside or an outside border or both to the worksheet or selection
Save and open files:	
Save this file	Saves current document
Open file	Opens My Documents folder <or default folder>

INTERNET EXPLORER COMMANDS REFERENCE SHEET

Say this:	**To do this:**
STARTING INTERNET EXPLORER	
Start Internet Explorer or Open Internet Explorer	Launch program
ADDRESS BAR	
Go to Address	Move to Address Bar and selects the contents
\<Dictate or spell out the web address\>	Insert web address into Address Bar
Go There or Click Go or Press Enter	Go to web address in Address Bar
FAVORITES	
Favorites or Display (or Show, View) Favorites	Open the Favorites list
Hide (or close) Favorites	Close the Favorites list
Add to Favorites	Open Add to Favorites dialogue box
Click \<Link Name\> or any words within an active link	Activate link (or numbers multiple links)
Show Links or Hide Links	Display Links Bar or Hide Links Bar
SCROLLING	
Start scrolling up or Start scrolling down	Start automatic scrolling
Speed Up or Slow Down (repeat to go faster/slower)	Increase or decrease scrolling speed
Stop Scrolling	Stop automatic scrolling
NAVIGATE WEB PAGES	
Move Up/Down \<n\>	Move page up specified number
Line Up or Line Down	Move page up or down 1 line
Page up or Page Down	Move up or down one screen
Go to Top or Go to Bottom	Move cursor to top or bottom of web page
Go Home	Return to Home Page
Go Back	Move back one screen
Go Forward	Move forward one screen
Stop Loading	Activate the Stop Button
Reload or Refresh	Refresh the page

Image or Click Image	Number the images with hidden links on screen
<Name of Button> or Click <Name of Button>	Activate button
Click Type Text or Click Edit Box	Move to and activate text box (or numbers multiple text boxes)
Click Check Box	Number all check boxes and go to first one
Choose <n>	Select the image, option, button, etc. from numbered list of choices
Click Radio Button or Radio Button	Number all radio button options and go to first one
Check List Box or List Box	Number all boxes with list of choices (drop down lists) and go to first one
Show Choices	Open a drop-down list of choices
Hide Choices	Close a drop-down list of choices
Click <Text>	Select an entry from a list of choices
Do a Search	Open Search Browser
Find a Word on this Page	Open Find dialog box
Open (or Expand, Drop) List	Open drop-down list

TIPS for Using Internet:

1. Your Web browser does not have to be open to start a Web search by voice. Dragon recognizes when you use a voice search command and opens your default browser for you. However, be sure you wait until entire page is loaded before giving commands or dictating. Also, watch screen to make sure your dictation or command has processed before making another command. Too many commands at once can cause the browser to freeze.

2. Fill in dialogue boxes by simply dictating into the box.

3. Press the Enter Key by saying "Press Enter"

4. Say "Click" anytime you want to choose an item on the web page or choose a link.

5. If more than one button matches your command, a series of numbered markers appear next to the possible matches.

6. Use the "Show Dictation Box" to dictate and transfer text when words don't seem to appear when dictating in specific locations.

   Remember, you can use the mouse and keyboard interchangeably with your voice at any time. Most people still prefer to navigate the web by using their keyboard or mouse. However, they prefer using their voice to chat or create e-mails.

For additional information and resources, use Dragon Help

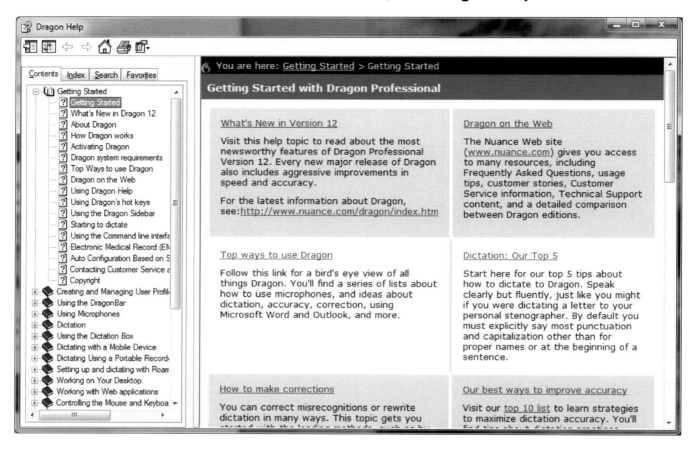

http://www.nuance.com/for-individuals/by-product/dragon-for-pc/existing-customers/index.htm

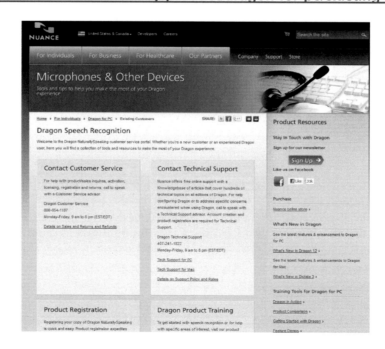

Terms of Use
Please read before accessing this information, either in print, online, or on CD.

This training manual contains instructional materials, documentation and other information related to products and services of Speaking Solutions Incorporated, a Nebraska-based corporation. (Also referred to as "SpeakingSolutions.com" or "Speaking Solutions"). This information is provided as a courtesy to customers of Speaking Solutions, Incorporated and those who have been trained by Speaking Solutions Incorporated consultants or trainers. By accessing or using any information contained herein, you agree to be bound by the terms and conditions described in these Terms of Use.

Copyright Notice

Other Intellectual Property Rights
Speaking Solutions, Incorporated, Speaking Solutions and SpeakingSolutions.com, and other names of Speaking Solutions products, product features, and services are the property of Speaking Solutions, Incorporated in the United States and other countries. Speaking Solutions, Incorporated also uses the following trademarks that are not currently registered with the USPTO. Some of these trademarks are the subject of trademark applications and may become registered in the future:

SpeakingSolutions.Com, Speaking Solutions, Nifty 50, Nifty 58, Nifty 59.
Other product and company names mentioned in this material, or on the web site, on CD or other printed materials are the trademarks of their respective owners. Nothing contained in these Terms of Use shall be construed as conferring by implication, estoppel, or any other legal theory, a license or right to any patent, trademark, copyright, or other intellectual property right, except those expressly provided herein. The products, processes, software, and other technology described may be the subject of other intellectual property rights owned by Speaking Solutions, Incorporated or by third parties.

Disclaimer

INDEX